EMILY WILDING DAVISON

D1363184

"Compelling, enraging and inspiring. Lucy Fisher reveals Emily Wilding Davison to have been a passionate and difficult woman whom it is impossible not to admire."
CAROLINE CRIADO PEREZ

"Lucy Fisher's compelling account of Emily Wilding Davison's struggle is a must-read. Her biography paints a vivid picture of an extraordinarily committed and radical suffragette who dedicated her life to the women's movement. I can't recommend this book enough – and would urge anyone interested in the feminist struggle to read it."
CAROLINE LUCAS MP

"At last! A biography of the suffragette martyr who emerged from the crowd to try to grab the bridle of King George V's horse at the 1913 Derby, symbolically reaching for the reins of power. Lucy Fisher's definitive and dashing narrative honours Emily Wilding Davison, who died for Votes for Women."
DIANE ATKINSON

"Emily Wilding Davison's qualities – total dedication to a controversial cause, preparedness to endure suffering and vilification, super-activism, almost supernatural resilience – these are the very qualities that today's generation of feminists need. This book sweeps you through her incredible life and leaves you certain that today she'd be at the forefront of modern women's struggles: #MeToo, the pay gap and the battle against domestic violence. A book for boys and men, too, to learn that women changed the world."
HARRIET HARMAN

"In Lucy Fisher's compelling narrative Emily Wilding Davison finds her ideal biographer. Here is the story of a courageous woman, intelligent, dedicated, uncompromising, told in sympathetic detail – warts and all. As I read of Davison's seven hunger strikes and the forty-nine times she was force-fed, I admired her bravery and was awed by her sustained militancy. We owe her much, and Lucy Fisher brings to her story a keen, appraising eye."
JOAN BAKEWELL

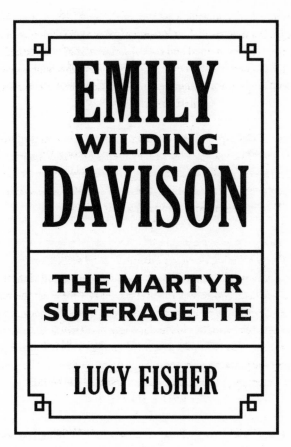

EMILY
WILDING
DAVISON

THE MARTYR SUFFRAGETTE

LUCY FISHER

Biteback Publishing

First published in Great Britain in 2018 by
Biteback Publishing Ltd
Westminster Tower
3 Albert Embankment
London SE1 7SP
Copyright © Lucy Fisher 2018

ISBN 978-1-78590-412-7

10 9 8 7 6 5 4 3 2 1

A CIP catalogue record for this book is available from the British Library.

Set in Adobe Caslon Pro

Printed and bound in Great Britain by
CPI Group (UK) Ltd, Croydon CR0 4YY

ACKNOWLEDGEMENTS

Thank you to my editor Stephanie Carey at Biteback Publishing for her thoughtful, intelligent and rigorous improvements to the text. Thanks also to Olivia Beattie and Iain Dale at Biteback for commissioning an expanded second edition of this biography in 2018 to coincide with the centenary anniversary of female enfranchisement, when women over the age of thirty with a property qualification won the vote.

My thanks also go to David Randall who used his unparalleled expertise to hone and edit the shorter first edition of this biography, which was written to mark the one-hundred-year anniversary of Emily Wilding Davison's death in 2013. David also helped conduct meticulous research into the suffragette's genealogy. Thanks too to his son, Simon Randall, who marketed the first edition of the book.

I would like to acknowledge the painstaking and important work conducted by Professor Carolyn Collette in transcribing Davison's archive, which is collated in her collection *In the Thick of the Fight: The Writing of Emily Wilding Davison, Militant Suffragette*. Thanks to the University of Michigan Press for approving the reprint in full of both an important speech and essay by Davison that were transcribed by Collette. I would also like to acknowledge historian Maureen Howes's contributions to uncovering the genealogy and local historical context of Davison's life and family in the north-east.

Anna Towlson, the archives and special collections group manager at the London School of Economics, and Colin Panter at Press Association were a great help in sourcing photographs. My thanks also go to Deborah Claire, the writer of *A Necessary Woman*, a play about Davison written in 2018, who identified and passed on to me a still from footage she uncovered of the suffragette at a demonstration in June 1910.

Finally I would like to say thank you to my mother Anne, father Angus and brother Jack Fisher for their interest, but most of all to my husband, Theo Barclay, for his ideas and patience.

CONTENTS

Introduction   1

Chapter 1   The Child of a Most Unusual Union,   11
             1872–1891

Chapter 2   A Formative Tragedy,   25
             1891–1906

Chapter 3   The Awakening of a Suffragette,   35
             1906–1909

Chapter 4   The Beginnings of Militancy,   49
             March–October 1909

Chapter 5   An Incident in Prison,   63
             October 1909–1910

Chapter 6   The Woman in Parliament,   83
             1910–1911

Chapter 7   The Torture of Force-Feeding,   111
             1911–1912

Chapter 8   A Near Brush with Death in Prison,   125
             June 1912

Chapter 9   'To Lay Down Life For Friends ...   137
             That Is Glorious', June 1912–June 1913

Chapter 10   An Intruder at the Derby,   167
             4–8 June 1913

Chapter 11   Suicide, Misadventure or Martyrdom?   189
             10–13 June 1913

Chapter 12   A Heroine in Death, a Martyr Thereafter   205

Appendix 1   'The Price of Liberty'   223

Appendix 2   Her Only Extant Speech   229

Appendix 3   'Incendiarism', 1911   243

Notes   263

Sources and Bibliography   267

About the Author   271

Index   273

INTRODUCTION

When Emily Wilding Davison arose on 4 June 1913, she was among the most prominent militants of her time. By sundown that evening she had committed the act that made her one of the most famous women of the twentieth century. One hundred years on from the first British women winning the franchise, it is easy to take for granted the rights for which she fought. She never wavered, however, in her determination to achieve women's suffrage, and after seven years of harsh struggle she had resolved to make a final stand.

The day had started in a low-key fashion. The forty-year-old activist left her south London lodgings and made her way to Victoria train station, where she caught a train to Epsom in Surrey. She was bound for the Derby – then, as now, one of the most anticipated days in the sporting season. Amid the thrumming crowds she waited for the main race of the afternoon, whiling away time – and perhaps attempting to avoid suspicion – by marking her race card. As the hour approached she took up a prime rail-side position at Tattenham Corner, where the sweeping downhill curve of the track meets the home straight. The race commenced and Davison steeled herself. The leading horses, grouped together tightly, shot past her. A second wave of horses trailed them. Without hesitation she bobbed under the rail and rushed out on the course. Her arms raised in front of her face, she leapt at the King's horse as it galloped towards her. She was hurled thirty feet upon impact, tumbling several rotations down the course. Eventually she landed in a broken heap on the turf, her hat cartwheeling in the other direction. Suffering a fractured skull and brain injuries, she died four days later.

Davison's sensation final act of protest, made in the name of women's suffrage, immediately won her a place in the annals and defined her persona in the public imagination. The notoriety of her demise, however, has tended to overshadow the story of her life. It is the tale of an extraordinary woman who emerged from the obscurity of a comfortable Victorian upbringing to become one of the most daring activists of her day. After enduring intense physical, mental and emotional suffering in pursuit of her cause, she finally determined that a tragic gesture was required to end her comrades' hardship.

Her childhood had been a gilded one, replete with an expensive education and a year spent in Switzerland. Davison may have expected an easy and affluent life ahead of her, but it was not to be. At age twenty, the death of her father saw her family unexpectedly plunged into penury. Her mother was forced to move north and earn a living by opening a small bakery, while Davison left full-time studies to seek employment as a teacher and then a governess.

By her early thirties she had served with a number of renowned families. Her attentions were increasingly diverted, however, by the campaign for female enfranchisement. In the United Kingdom the suffragists had been calling in earnest for votes for women since the 1870s. By the turn of the century several different groups had collapsed into the National Union of Women's Suffrage Societies, led by Millicent Fawcett. They advocated a respectful, constitutionalist approach based on lobbying for political reform through meetings with politicians.

Davison, however, joined a new and more aggressive group: the Women's Social and Political Union. Founded by Emmeline Pankhurst in 1903, and led by her and her daughters Christabel and Sylvia, the suffragettes, as they were branded by the *Daily Mail*, resolved to oppose the government through direct action.

Every reformist movement requires its protagonists to inhabit a cast of roles and the WSPU was no different. Alongside the charismatic leadership there were strategists, organisers, fixers, donors and proselytisers. Davison tried her hand at the last role, making a number of addresses to activist meetings and writing prolifically in support of the movement. Despite her extensive written output – comprising letters to newspapers, criticism of contemporary arts and essays – in the end she placed more faith in the sentiment embodied by the movement's motto: 'Deeds not words'.

Her pivotal role, then, was one that is crucial to all radical causes: that of the agitator willing to transgress the conventions of polite society and the strictures of the law. Her direct action – comprising arson campaigns, vandalism and assault – landed her in prison nine times. During these periods of incarceration she undertook numerous hunger strikes and was subjected to the ordeal of force-feeding on almost fifty occasions. Hers was not an easy part to play, entailing, as it did, sharp bursts of agonising pain, long-term ill health and psychological trauma. Longueurs in solitary confinement, during which she and her comrades communicated only via overheard screams and groans as they were forcibly pumped with liquid nutrition, took their toll on her mental state. The suffering she and her allies endured, designed in part to weaken the movement, had the opposite effect – only entrenching her commitment to the cause. As the torment worsened, her conviction of the urgent need for progress deepened.

Davison's devotion to the cause propelled her through the ranks of the WSPU to rise from a protest steward in 1908 to a dauntless militant entrusted with secret missions a year later. In time, her ferocity and recalcitrance proved too much, however, even for the Pankhursts. A wildcard rebel, she became ostracised from the central command and forced out to the fringes of the movement.

She never vacillated in her belief that she, and all her sex,

were honour-bound to struggle in pursuit of the vote, itself
the starting point from which every other form of societal
gender discrimination could be fought. All women should
sacrifice to the level they felt able, she wrote: their 'livelihood,
position, wealth, friends, relatives and, not least common,
[risk of] loss of health or even possibly life'.

To this end Davison forfeited the prospect of marriage or
romance, children, employment and security. Her forbear-
ance was heroic and she rarely spoke of the personal impact
it entailed, revealing only on one occasion, with candour, the
'personal shrinking a woman feels as a matter of certainty
after being thrust into publicity'.

Shunned widely by peers and acquaintances for her association with militancy, her sometimes overbearing nature
could rankle with colleagues. In time, however, she built up
a network of close comrades, for whom she demonstrated a
striking capacity for warmth and loyalty. They, in turn, cared
deeply for their friend and her safety, eventually beseeching
her to step back from the frontline of the movement, insist-
ing she had done enough.

She also relied on her faith, which provided comfort in
times of difficulty. Moreover, it was her steadfast certainty in
the God-ordained righteousness of the movement, and her
role in it, that had underscored her initial adoption of militant tactics. The recurring Christian theme of self-sacrifice
inspired a deep desire to emulate Christ by giving up her
life for others. The same trope drove her fixation with Joan
of Arc, the quintessential female warrior and Christian

martyr who had been adopted by the suffrage movement as a spiritual figurehead.

The concept of martyrdom preoccupied Davison's thoughts more and more in the last months of her life. After years of broken promises from politicians and false starts in the House of Commons, where a series of franchise bills had been introduced but then stalled, she anticipated that a change of direction was required to achieve a breakthrough. As the authorities learnt how to deal with the suffragettes with minimum fuss or publicity, the two sides had reached an impasse. A major shock was needed to jolt the government and the public out of its inertia. That was Davison's conclusion when she headed to Epsom Derby that bright day in June 1913.

Her final act was meticulously planned to reach the widest possible audience. The event itself was likely chosen because the famous bystanders – not only politicians and aristocrats, but the King and Queen themselves – attracted the entire nation's press. In addition, the precise spot Davison picked to intrude on the racecourse was one on which all the camera lenses would be trained. Newsreel technology, which had only been developed two years earlier, captured her protest on film. The shocking, macabre footage of the collision was shown in theatres in the aftermath, and it gripped the country. It was one of the first times that a radical movement had harnessed arresting imagery to such effect.

Davison's legacy has evolved over time and in the immediate wake of her death she was leapt upon by the Pankhursts and reclaimed as one of their own. The WSPU pronounced her a martyr and convened a grand funeral procession through the streets of London. The suffragette press published her essay 'Price of Liberty' and a hagiographic short biography. She was held aloft as the movement's very own Joan of Arc: the tireless militant, chosen by God, who had been prepared to give her life for the cause.

Horror and awe characterised the response of the British establishment. The derision and scorn that had been heaped on Davison by many commentators during her lifetime escalated following her death. Her perceived indifference towards the jockey and horse – both of whom she could have killed – was widely reviled. In the minds of many, her act had been a terrible deed and she herself a mad, hysterical and dangerous woman. Even some suffragist groups disowned her act, believing it to have damaged their cause, and declined to attend her funeral.

The suffragettes' violent direct action remains controversial to this day, with historians divided over the ethics and efficacy of the campaign. Davison herself grappled with the subject, but surmised that after forty years of 'untiring, devoted effort' by the suffragists without effect, 'a change of method was necessary'. Militancy had been successful in catapulting the issue of female enfranchisement to the top of the political agenda, she later maintained.

Many suffrage sympathisers nonetheless argued to the contrary: that the strategy only served to stiffen public and political opposition to the cause. The criminal offences undertaken by the boldest suffragettes convinced some members of the public that women could not be trusted with a vote. For many of Davison's contemporaries, the risk posed to innocent human lives, and the damage done to private and public property, could not be justified. A slump in WSPU membership and a decline in commercial activities linked to merchandise around the movement coincided with an escalation in its militancy from 1912 onwards, suggesting that heightened aggression damaged the battle for hearts and minds. Furthermore, critics insisted that whatever the nation's sentiments, the government could not allow itself to be seen to back down in the face of militancy.

In modern times the suffragettes are seen as having been on the right side of history, struggling towards a goal that would always, in time, have won out. Women now have voting rights in almost every country in the world and even nations like Saudi Arabia that have dragged their feet have been forced to begin to catch up with modernity. While the activists' reputations have been rehabilitated to a degree, it is striking that when it came to celebrating the centenary anniversary of the first wave of women winning the vote in 2018, it was Fawcett, the leader of the peaceable suffragists, rather than one of the Pankhursts – let alone Davison – who was commemorated with a statue in Parliament Square. Nonetheless, the banner held up by the larger-than-life bronze sculpture harks back to Davison's sacrifice, reprising a line from Fawcett's tribute to the martyr suffragette: 'Courage calls to courage everywhere'.

A movement has arisen in recent years calling for all the suffragettes imprisoned around the turn of the century, who numbered about 1,000, to be posthumously pardoned for their crimes. The request, while well-intentioned, misunderstands the point of their militancy, however. Arrests, court appearances and jail sentences were all a core plank of the suffragettes' strategy, not only to publicise their cause, but also to demonstrate the seriousness of their intent.

Davison's death, like the First World War, became a major milestone on the long road towards female enfranchisement. It has continued to inspire future generations, and countless artworks have been created, and plays and poetry written, to retell and commemorate her story.

It is worth considering what her legacy would have been, however, if she had survived her act of protest at the Derby. Would she have lain down arms at the beginning of the Great War, as the WSPU directed its followers to do, or would she have continued to battle on until she had been fully disowned by the group? Her attitude in the last few months suggests that she may not have got that far. Whether in June 1913 or shortly afterwards, she was, as a pious and uncompromising radical, committed to making the ultimate sacrifice in the name of women and of God.

Davison idealised the 'perfect amazon, who will sacrifice unto the last for the freedom of her sex'. As she put it: 'To lay down life for friends, that is glorious, selfless, inspiring! But to re-enact the tragedy of Calvary for generations yet unborn, that is the last consummate sacrifice of the Militant!'

CHAPTER 1

THE CHILD OF A MOST UNUSUAL UNION 1872–1891

E mily Wilding Davison was born in 1872 of a strange union. Her father, Charles Edward Davison, was fifty years old and her mother Margaret was just nineteen when the two wed. He was an affluent, worldly widower with a brood of nine children in tow while she was his teenage housekeeper.

Charles had been raised by his parents in a comfortable middle-class household in Alnwick, Northumberland. Urbane, well educated and adventurous, he travelled extensively and lived abroad for many years during the early part of his life, and also ran a number of successful businesses. Before the death of Sarah Seton Chisholm, his first wife, Charles had been happily married for eighteen years and had seen the eldest of his nine children leave home to train as a lawyer. He had, therefore, already lived a fulfilled life before he set eyes on Margaret, who, as a young member of the household staff, had seen little of the world.

Margaret Caisley was from a modest background. Despite being born only twenty miles south of the town of Charles's birth, she came from a different world. Local Northumberland archives list her as 'the daughter of a Gentleman', but this was an overstatement for a girl forced to leave her family home while still a teenager to seek a living as a housekeeper. In reality, Margaret's father was a publican who owned a small inn, The White Swan, in the market town of Morpeth, which lies on the River Wansbeck. With her father unable to support his daughter financially through adulthood, Margaret was forced to take up a service position in Charles Davison's elegant household.

The union, unorthodox but by no means unprecedented in Victorian society, suited both parties. Charles, accustomed to bounding around the country on business-related tours, found himself sole carer to his children following his first wife's death. The younger members of his extensive progeny required a nurturing mother figure and Margaret, with youthful energy, was effortlessly pitched into the role of stepmother. In only a few years she had been elevated from her role as servant to mistress of the house, with a staff of five to supervise.

Margaret's background contrasted starkly with that of Charles's first wife, who had been born into a family of rich colonial settlers. Both Charles and Sarah were born in 1822, he in England, she in Calcutta, India. In his early twenties, Charles had left the northern skies of his birth and headed for the subcontinent, pursuing the promise of fortune in what was then deemed exotic frontierland. His boldness was rewarded and, like many Englishmen who ventured into the heart of the empire in the nineteenth century, he swiftly became a successful merchant. Charles married his young love in Simla in 1848 in what, if it had followed the convention of their time and standing, would likely have been a majestic ceremony. The pair had three children in India before returning to England in 1854, around the time their eldest son, Charles Chisholm, turned five years old.

With the wealth Charles had amassed, the family bought Winton House, a manor house in Morpeth which later became a Freemasons' hall. Only their youngest son was born there, however. Before 1864, census records indicate that the family spent the majority of time in another property – Warblington House in Emsworth, Hampshire, near the border with West Sussex. Always in pursuit of novel business opportunities, Charles spent time in London and put money into a tramway company. The investment would prove in time to be a foolhardy move.

The couple wanted a large family and by 1864 Sarah had given birth to her ninth baby, John Anderson, fifteen years after her first child was born. Just two years later Sarah, who had long suffered ill health, suddenly died, aged only forty-four. Charles was now faced with the prospect of raising his young family alone. By this time several of their children were about to leave home and embark on adult life; the pair's eldest son, Charles, was to train in law, and would go on to establish a legal practice in London. Yet the youngest were still infants and it is likely Charles realised they required care, attention and maternal influence that he alone could not provide.

He did not have to look far for his eyes to alight on his young housekeeper. In 1867, within two years of her arrival in the house, Margaret became pregnant. In February the following year, her first child Letitia was born and in the August she and Charles married. Soon after, a second child, Alfred, was born. Emily would be the third of Margaret's four offspring. Her striking middle name derived, improbably, from the father of Charles's first wife, whom she had never met. George Wilding Chisholm, the maternal grandfather of Emily's half-siblings, had been a successful merchant in Calcutta, where he lived until his death in 1843.

Although Margaret and Charles were married in Greenwich in August 1868, they were still living in the north at the time of Alfred's birth in May 1869. It is notable that Charles, Margaret, and later Emily herself, all felt the irresistible pull of the north-east – though they had left for London, they were all eventually compelled to return to the land of their forebears. Charles and Margaret made one sortie south after Alfred's birth and took up residency with their assortment of young and teenage children in Greenwich. This chaotic mix, comprising an oddly matched couple, a sister and brother in infancy, and a host of growing and grown half-siblings was the family into which Emily was born on a cold, wet Friday morning in October 1872.

Margaret gave birth in Blackheath, south-east London. It is fitting that Emily was born in the capital, for her heart remained in her metropolitan birth town – to which she would later write paeans – throughout the rest of her life, although a strong affinity with Northumberland evolved over time too. Like her mother, who later retired to the northern county, Emily's life would follow a northwards path and the north-eastern village of Morpeth would become her final resting place.

Emily was baptised at the age of two months in St Alfege's, Greenwich, a handsome Hawksmoor-designed Anglican church. Her christening was significant in marking the beginning of a relationship with religion that would underpin the narrative of her life. Her devotion to Christianity deepened as she grew older and her religious conviction provided the moral backdrop to her practical and theoretical feminism. Emily's participation in the struggle for women's suffrage became inextricably intertwined with her theology. Forty years after her baptism in Greenwich, it was, in the end, a religious fervour that fuelled her final moments at Epsom.

Her first months were couched in the smart surrounds of Roxburgh House, a spacious property on Vanbrugh Park Road which neighbours the expansive green pastures of Greenwich Park. While the Davison family moved often throughout Emily's childhood, affluence and urban luxury remained the standard. The opposite would define the circumstances of her adult life, which was characterised by sparsity and financial struggle.

From Greenwich the Davison family moved to Saw-bridgeworth, a charming village straddling Hertfordshire and Essex. There they purchased Gaston House, described by Gertrude Colmore,[i] who wrote a brief contemporary biography of Emily, as 'a Georgian house three stories in height, with tall, spacious rooms, and on its red brick front the kindly look that some old houses have.' Emily was educated by a resident governess, attesting to the Davison family's wealth during those early years. She lived there happily until the age of nine.

Colmore's biography, which was published by The Women's Press in 1913 shortly after Emily's death, provides the only detailed account of the suffragette's early years. It is a political work that was designed as propaganda for the women's suffrage movement and encouraged the view of the suffragette as a martyr for the cause. Despite its breathless tone and sometimes hagiographic perspective, it is useful for its testimony from Emily's friends about her character and intransigent nature.

One telling vignette depicted her nurse calling her in from the garden and asking that she be a good girl. Emily responded obstinately: 'I don't want to be good.' It is clear from the evidence collected by Colmore that Emily's environment during the early years of her life provided an emotionally

---

i   Gertrude Colmore was the pen name of Gertrude Baillie-Weaver, a writer
     and feminist. She and her husband Harold were notable supporters of
     animal rights. The statue 'The Shepherdess', in Regent's Park, London, was
     erected in their honour by the National Council for Animal Welfare in 1931.

secure and nurturing setting for her development. What developed, right from the start, was not a demure, compliant character, as was expected of women of that era, but a more strong-willed personality. Emily's cast-iron stubbornness and her taste for mischievousness seem to have begun early.

She was particularly close to her younger sister Ethel, who was less than two years her junior. The two young girls shared a bedroom during their early childhood and would giggle and sing hymns together after they were put to bed. It was behaviour that showed a combination of aspects of Emily's character: pious yet capable of being unruly. She never changed – years later, she would sing and chant verses from the same hymns while locked in prison cells up and down the country.

In many ways she was a playful child and she gained a nickname for her roguish precocity. She would angle for treats from adults, brazenly demanding 'Weet! Weet!', aware that her endearing lisp meant she could not pronounce 'sweet' correctly. The name 'Weet' stuck, and well into her thirties Emily would sign postcards to her mother using the name.

She earned another nickname in childhood that spoke to the more difficult, awkward side of her tough personality. Once, when playing at soldiers, Colmore says she riled her young friends with her demanding perfectionism. She sulkily withdrew from the game when the soldiers were assembled for marching in an incorrect order and her obstinacy spoiled the game for the rest. They resentfully chanted 'Pem' at her, a word in the group's made-up child-language that expressed their anger. 'Pem', like 'Weet', caught on, and eventually assumed a tone of affection rather than displeasure when her friends addressed her by the childhood moniker.[ii] Still, a willingness even at that young, impressionable age, to take a stand against consensus, no matter how uncomfortable or provocative, was evident.

Overall, Emily was remembered by her peers as a high-spirited and daring child. A friend with whom she would go and stay in Lancashire said that there was 'nothing mean or small about her. Always very affectionate and impulsive, and, needless to say, a most intelligent child'. Emily hated being teased, which, 'as she was one of a large family, happened not too rarely'. She took herself seriously and disdained jokes at her own expense.

Yet, while there was little obvious reason for such occasional dourness, when she was seven, Emily's carefree childhood was dealt a shocking blow. Her beloved six-year-old sister Ethel suddenly died. There was a mere nineteen-month gap between the two and they had been inseparable. Emily had been so protective and tender towards Ethel that the rest of the family called her 'little mother'. Her grief was profound, and a lasting sense of loss remained a heavy presence throughout the rest of her life.

Ethel was interred in the family plot in Morpeth churchyard, where Emily would later be buried too – another

---

ii   She also used the nickname 'Pem' to mark photographic portraits of herself and to sign off postcards to friends and family.

premature death in the Davison family. Ethel's grave can still be seen today in the grounds of the church; the epitaph reads:

IN LOVING MEMORY OF DARLING ETHEL
Died 24th July 1880
Age: Six Years

Emily was encouraged to take comfort from her intense grief in prayer. The Davisons were a devout, church-going family and Emily was inspired by Christian scripture from a young age. The passing of Ethel gave meaning to a fledgling faith that would eventually verge on fanatical fervour.

In addition to the religious tone of Emily's upbringing, her family life had bearing on her later beliefs in other ways too. The varying backgrounds of Emily's parents may have opened her eyes to the spectrum of experience across the class divides of Victorian society. She would have been aware that her mother came from a poor enough background to warrant her domestic servitude while still a teenager. Further back through Emily's ancestry on her mother's side, her great-grandmother, Dorothy Donaldson, died widowed and poor in Bedlington, Northumberland after raising nine children. The poverty central to Emily's heritage on her mother's side would likely have inspired empathy in the sensitive young woman, who demonstrated a strong sense of justice from an early age. As Maureen Howes, a Morpeth historian and genealogist who has also written a biography of Emily Wilding Davison, explained: 'Seeing her life through her family history puts an entirely different perspective on it ... Emily lived in two social worlds: her father's upper middle class world in London and her mother's quieter, rural, working class world of Northumberland.'

Few extant sources attest to Charles's treatment of his young, working-class wife. What is certain is that as she grew older Emily became well attuned to the social injustices working-class women faced and she became a committed combatant in the fight for the advancement and protection of female workers. The disparity in legal rights between men and women became a specific focus of concern to which she returned repeatedly in her writing.

When she was eleven years old, the Davison family moved from Gaston House back to the heart of London. In contrast to their smart residence in leafy Greenwich some years earlier, Charles was forced to choose a shabbier house for his family, this time in the neighbourhood of Fulham. Although bordering the Royal Borough of Kensington and Chelsea, the property at 42 Fairholme Road in West Kensington was markedly more modest than the Davisons' previous homes. Money was getting tight. Nonetheless, having completed her elementary education under the auspices of a governess, Emily went on to enrol in Miss Crookshank's day school in Kensington. It was the kind of smart preparatory school that had sprung up to cater for young ladies from the new urban-dwelling middle classes that had evolved in the industrial revolution. Her siblings were educated in similar establishments – Emily's older brother Alfred started as a boarder at a private school in Suffolk, Crespigny House School, in 1881.

After a year at Miss Crookshank's, Emily spent twelve months in Dunkirk with one of her sisters (it is likely to have been a half-sister, whom she would continue to visit throughout her life). Emily would come to welcome the anonymity and restorative change of surroundings that France provided when recovering from prison stints years after that first sojourn in the country. Spending time on the continent and learning a European language demonstrates the kind of privileged environment in which she grew up, and the aspirations her father harboured for her. A year in France or Italy was considered vital credentials for a prospective well-to-do wife, and securing a good husband was no doubt at the forefront of Charles's mind. Emily greatly enjoyed practising French and had a proficient aptitude for languages. Her school reports tell of good achievement in German and she later obtained a degree in modern languages in London.

In 1885, at the age of thirteen, Emily returned from France and enrolled at Kensington High School. She would study there until 1891, apart from a year spent in Lausanne, Switzerland, where she consolidated her French language skills. All her school reports document the enthusiasm, verve and perseverance that characterised her militant behaviour later on in life. She is said to have fared 'better in examinations than expected' and shown 'thought and originality above the average'.

Her headmistress Agnes Hitchcock took a particular interest in the teenage pupil. She later wrote:

I well remember Emily coming with her father, who was evidently very devoted to her and very much afraid she might be over-worked. She was a rather delicate looking child, fair-haired and without much colour, but with bright, intelligent eyes, and a half shy, half confident way of looking up with her head a little on one side and smiling at one which won my heart at once. She seemed, I remember, delighted to be coming to school and to be with other girls, and that is my impression of her all the time she was there; her pleasure in her work and her interest in everything that went on.

Hitchcock and her pupil remained in contact after the latter left the school and developed a lasting friendship.

Interestingly, one of Davison's schoolfellows said that she was 'law-abiding by nature', commenting that she was the curious reverse 'of the aggressive character generally expected of the suffragette – made or in the making'.[1]

By all accounts she was a good-natured and agreeable, if high-spirited, woman throughout her adult life. Far from being rebellious or lawless, it was only the strength of her beliefs in the righteousness of the women's suffrage movement that propelled her towards militancy in her mid-thirties. Davison's religious conviction provided her with the strength to overcome the naturally assenting, eager-to-please aspect of her character that accompanied her wilfulness.

Beyond modern languages, Davison had a passion for English literature. She was enchanted by the works of Chaucer and consequently adopted the Middle English sobriquet 'Faire Emelye' among her friends. A school report from that time states: 'She was an interesting pupil, quickly stirred over passages in history and literature that appealed to her sense of the noble and the beautiful. Under a quiet, unassuming exterior there was a great fund of enthusiasm, and a surprising power of steady and persistent work.' It was similarly a perception of the beauty and nobility of the women's suffrage cause that later inspired her whole-hearted commitment to it. She later saw virtue in the sacrifice that she and her comrades were making for the benefit of all women, and grace in the close relationships she enjoyed with her allies, describing friendship as 'one of the priceless jewels of life' that held 'inestimable riches'.

Although bright, she was not endowed with genius in her early school years, or even the easy facility for rising to the top of the class that some children have. Rather it was her perseverance and conscientiousness that led her to academic success. Agnes Hitchcock said of Emily in a reference supplied on her behalf in 1894:

Her school career was in all respects highly satisfactory. She gave evidence of good abilities and of a power of steady persevering work that made her teachers augur well of her future. The subjects in which she did remarkably well here, were, French, English Literature and Drawing … My knowledge of her enables me to say with confidence that she would prove earnest, diligent and conscientious in any work that she undertook.

Aside from schoolwork, Emily enjoyed cycling, skating and dancing – the athletic activities suitable for a young woman from a prosperous family in the final decades of the nineteenth century. She excelled at swimming and at the Chelsea Baths swimming championship she gained a gold medal after which she was offered the opportunity to turn professional when a champion spotted her swimming in Brighton. She declined. Colmore also notes: 'At Cromer[iii] one season she was the last of the bathers, bathing well on into November.' It was, perhaps, an early indication of the kind of physical hardiness she was to demonstrate later in life when suffering through multiple prison sentences.

In addition to an interest in outdoor pursuits, Emily enjoyed the theatre. It was a hobby that became more complex in later years, when the suffragettes conceived the idea of headline-grabbing arson attacks on West End theatres. Her dramatic tastes were wide-roaming, and she once declared to a companion, perhaps dismissive of an invitation to a lowbrow comedy: 'My tastes are far more catholic than yours for I can enjoy a musical comedy as much as a Shakespeare play or a Bernard Shaw or a Gilbert Murray.'[iv]

---

iii   A coastal town in Norfolk.
iv   A feted translator of classical Greek drama.

CHAPTER 2

A FORMATIVE TRAGEDY
1891–1906

I n 1891, at the age of nineteen, Emily passed the Oxford and Cambridge Higher School Certificate. This achievement helped her win a place at Holloway College (later Royal Holloway), fulfilling a dream she had nursed since visiting the grounds with a school friend several years before. The women-only college had been founded by Thomas Holloway, a Victorian entrepreneur, just twelve years earlier. His wife had persuaded him to spend some money he had set aside for a philanthropic project on a new educational establishment reserved for women. Coincidentally, Holloway College shared the name of another institution thirty miles away at which Davison would spend time later on in life: Holloway Prison in north London.

Enrolling in 1892, Davison read for a combined degree in English language, literature and mathematics. All seemed set for the high-achieving young woman, but halfway through her studies, in February 1893, her father Charles – past seventy years old but outwardly sprightly – died unexpectedly. Amid the family's grief, Margaret and her children learnt that Charles had left them the pitiful sum of £102 1s 4d, an amount equivalent to less than £10,000 today. It was barely enough for the large family to subsist on for a matter of months, let alone sustain in perpetuity the lifestyle to which they had become accustomed.

During his life, Charles had displayed enough wealth to warrant description in the Morpeth Parish Register as 'A Gentleman of Independent Means'. It is also known that he continued to travel widely for business after his return from India – contemporary records describe him making frequent trips to Sweden, as well as throughout the UK. From a census result in 1891, it is also clear, however, that the family was in rather more reduced circumstances than they had once enjoyed. In 1871, Charles's household had five servants. By 1891, the retinue was reduced to a single maid, something even well-paid City clerks could afford. This maid was Lucy Abbey, a 25-year-old hailing from Morcott, Rutland. Charles himself was listed in that year's census as a 'Commission Agent', suggesting a relaxed profession in which he earned revenue from the profit margins of other businesses.

It is unclear exactly how the small fortune Charles had amassed throughout his life had dissipated by the time of his death. He had invested heavily in his son William's tramway companies and had poured money into patenting tram mechanisms. The *London Gazette* recorded a patent granted to Charles in November 1881, for example, for the invention of 'improvements in apparatus or appliances for stopping and restarting tramway-cars, carriages, and other like vehicles'. It is characteristic of Charles, a businessman with a keen sense of adventure, to have taken a chance on an exciting, but risky, investment prospect, such as new tramway technology. The poor return on investments in many British rail projects at the end of the nineteenth century may provide a clue as to the dissolution of Charles's wealth. Recent research has shown that major British railway companies suffered declining returns after 1897, with their share prices steadily falling. It is also possible that a large part of whatever estate he had possessed came from his widow Sarah and that, on his death, that money was left to her children, and not to Emily's branch of the family.

Most of Charles's children by his first wife, Sarah, had moved out by the time of his death, but Letitia still lived at home with Margaret, and Emily, aged twenty, was only halfway through her further education at Holloway College.

While she was studying her mother was forced to give up the family's London townhouse and return to the north-east to find a cheaper property. The little money left by Charles after his death soon dwindled and Margaret could no longer afford to live without working. She returned to the village of Longhorsley near her hometown of Morpeth, and, in her mid-forties, opened a bakery. The property it occupied was modest – part of the village's corner shop, opposite a pub.

Still, Margaret was resilient and appeared happy to bake and sell bread and cakes. Though this was an enterprising solution, the bakery did not turn over enough revenue to pay for the remainder of Emily's expensive education at Holloway, where the fees cost £20 each term.

Emily's anxiety about her future education was revealed in a letter she wrote to a friend on 15 February 1893, just after her father's funeral:

> *Today we have been very busy, and I have been out for Mamma. She has decided that I am to return tomorrow to college. It is very hard to leave them all, but what can one do? Mamma has to pay £20 a term for me, and it must not be wasted. I do not know whether I can stay on after this term, as we do not know how matters are yet, so I must make the best of this term. Mamma is very anxious to keep me at college for my exam if it is possible.*

In the event, staying on at Holloway was not a viable possibility and she was forced to leave. The principal, Ms M. E. Bishop, confirmed in a reference for Davison dated June that year that she had 'kept five terms here and is now obliged by family circumstances to leave College in the middle of her preparation for the Oxford Final School of English Language and Literature'.

Ms Bishop continued:

She has already taken the Oxford Pass Examination in

French, German, and English, with distinction in the last. Miss Davison possesses considerable activity and great energy and perseverance. She is courteous and good-natured in her relations to all about her. I feel sure that she will discharge whatever duties she undertakes vigorously and conscientiously.

The reference even noted in passing that 'she respects authority' – an irony given her later actions.

A month later came a further lament at the turn of events, this time from her English tutor, Ms. L. M. Faithfull. She wrote:

It is a matter of great regret to me that [Emily] is unable to finish her course at College, as I had every reason to think she would do well in her final examination. She is a most hard-working and enthusiastic student, and one whom it has always been a pleasure to teach from her real love of her subject. She has made decided progress during her time at College. She has immense perseverance and energy in overlooking obstacles, and spares no pains to make her work satisfactory. She has read widely and intelligently, and her power of criticism has developed. As a teacher of English Literature Miss Davison would, I am sure, be most thorough, and is quite competent to teach advanced pupils.

After two years at the college therefore, when she was only

halfway through her course, the promising twenty-year-old student left with a brave smile and good will. She knew she must find a job, but vowed to continue studying for her honours degree in her spare time. She took up a position as a governess, but brokered a provision to be given time for evening study alongside her daily duties. Unable to keep up without tutorial supervision, but resourceful, she borrowed lecture notes from friends still at the college. Eventually she saved up enough money to spend one term at St Hugh's Hall, a college at Oxford University founded in 1886 by Elizabeth Wordsworth, the great-niece of the poet William Wordsworth, for female students.[v] In April 1895 Davison took up her place there and excelled.

At the end of that term, Elizabeth Lea, a tutor presiding over female students at the university, wrote of her:

> She is a most industrious and painstaking student, and one who takes a real interest in her work. She has well deserved the great success she has just achieved.

That success was first class honours in English Language and Literature final examinations. Longhorsley legend has it that on the day Emily found out the result of her exams, she raced into her mother's shop, grabbed a glass jar of Black Bullets (popular peppermint-flavoured boiled sweets), and

---

v   The hall, later known as St Hugh's College, did not accept male students until 1986, its centenary year.

leapt around on the village green throwing them up in the air for delighted local children to catch.[2]

Women were not at that time admitted to degrees at Oxford; the university was immoveable on the issue until 1920. Even academics such as Elizabeth Lea, who was both a lecturer and tutor, were not admitted to doctorates, let alone professorial titles. The situation outraged Davison, justly proud of her excellent result. The perverse refusal of the University of Oxford to award women official certification or accreditation after undertaking the same studies as men was mirrored in the workplace, where women were not generally admitted to professional occupations such as law or medicine.

Undeterred by this discrimination, Davison strove to undertake a second degree, from the more enlightened London University where she matriculated as an external student in 1902. She was awarded a Bachelor of Arts degree with honours and, six years after her matriculation, also graduated with a third-class degree in modern languages. While her perfectionism and commitment would ordinarily have transformed her average aptitude for languages into a roaring academic success, this anomalous poor result must be partially attributable to the devotion with which Davison had begun applying herself to the women's suffrage cause by that juncture.

She financed her studies by working as a schoolmistress, as her former English teacher had recommended. In 1895 she had begun a role at the Church of England College for Girls at Edgbaston in Birmingham. Davison found the position exasperating; she could ill tolerate slow children and her impatience led to her moving on to find another post after just a year. Perhaps her resentment was obvious to the staff with whom she worked because, in August 1896, the headmistress of the school, Ms L. Landon Thomas, wrote in a reference: 'It suited me better not to keep Miss Davison on our staff, but to engage a second Science Mistress in her place.'

The prickly tone of the recommendation was diluted by her admission that 'Miss Davison ... is an enthusiast in her own subjects, and her students worked with interest and pleasure ... Before joining our staff she had had no experience of schoolwork, and she improved very much in her management of a Form and in discipline while with us.' Tellingly, she added: 'I consider Miss Davison better suited for girls in the middle and upper School than for quite young ones.'

She patently preferred teaching older children, and in particular, those in possession of a good degree of intelligence, rather than primary school infants. But throughout her year at the school, she was not particularly very happy. She was intolerant of laziness and found it hard to maintain discipline.

In 1886 her hunt for another paid position took her to Sussex, where she became a teacher for two years at Seabury School, West Worthing. This environment suited her better and she stayed there for two years, eventually earning enough money to pay for her further education. Again she earned an acceptable, albeit not glowing, reference from the school's head teacher: 'Miss Davison has been teaching in my school for the last two years, and has given me entire satisfaction. I have found her a most capable teacher, a conscientious worker, and a good disciplinarian.'

After graduating from the University of London as an external student, Davison obtained a post teaching the children of a family in Berkshire. She remained as their resident governess for six years. Rebecca West later noted that despite what she termed, in typical hagiographic fashion, Emily's 'pyrotechnic intelligence', she continued to bounce between insecure teaching positions for several years. None of them were at the level for which her education had prepared her.[3]

Between 1898 and 1909, then, Emily was a full-time teacher of one sort or another – either engaged as a school mistress or employed as a private governess. In 1901, records show she was working as a governess in Northamptonshire for a man called Edward Moorhouse and his family. There she taught fifteen-year-old Ann, eleven-year-old Mary and eight-year-old Edward Rhodes[vi] – a handful for a young woman, but not, Davison felt, a stimulating one.

In 1903, while she was living a slow-paced life in the countryside, Emmeline Pankhurst, the best-known pioneer of the women's suffrage movement, was busy founding a new organisation in Manchester: the Women's Political and Social Union (WSPU). Her daughter Christabel would become a

---

vi   Incidentally, an elder brother of her charges, William Rhodes-Moorhouse, became, in 1915, the first airman to be awarded the Victoria Cross.

bastion of the movement and in 1905 the younger Pankhurst began a programme of militancy. Christabel and fellow suffragist Annie Kenney disrupted the speeches of Winston Churchill and Sir Edward Grey, two of the most prominent politicians of that time, at a rally. Infiltrating the crowds, the duo heckled the speakers, calling out and demanding to know their views on women's political rights.

Such vociferous interruption was unheard of in polite Edwardian society. The obstreperous pair proceeded to unfurl a banner reading 'Votes for Women', which was to become the key slogan of the movement, along with 'Deeds not Words'. They were later arrested for assaulting a policeman. Both women refused to pay their fines and chose instead to serve a prison sentence. Their aim had been to gain publicity in the national newspapers and they succeeded.

Although Emily Wilding Davison may have been little aware of it then, a new era of militancy in the struggle for women's suffrage had dawned, and she was to become its foremost insurgent.

CHAPTER 3

THE AWAKENING OF A SUFFRAGETTE
1906–1909

W omen who lived in the first decades of the twentieth century were, in the eyes of the law and of wider society, non-participants in any matter of importance. The caveat was Queen Victoria, who presided over an empire stretching across a third of the globe until her death in 1901. Ordinary female citizens, however, had few rights and while wealthy, property-owning, single women had been allowed to cast a ballot in local council elections since a change in the law in 1869, none had a vote in national elections. As far as governance of the country was concerned, they did not count. Significant obstacles stood in the way of women who wanted to work in the professions and the conditions for unskilled workers were poor. Married women were *de facto* regarded as the property of their husbands and their fate was likely to entail repeated pregnancies.

The term 'birth control' was not dreamt up until 1914, and for many years after was not deemed a fit subject for public discourse. Nothing captured the subservient position of women better than the high fashion of the later Edwardian years – the tight, narrow, ankle-length dress known as the 'hobble skirt' which forced its wearers to walk in elegant, tiny steps. Women were often infantilised and chivalry was deployed as a means to condescend them. Davison herself took issue with this treatment in a letter to the *Sunday Times* in 1911, in which she said of the practice of men giving up their seats for women in a tram or railway-car:

> This form of chivalry is so debased that it is generally limited only to the young, the pretty, and the well-dressed, and so can be at once dismissed. This and many of the so-called marks of chivalry are generally governed by a false standard, which makes a man think that if he makes himself conspicuous by lifting his hat, or giving up his seat, or any other of the little points which mark that he is condescending, the more important duties of life can be ignored.[4]

An intelligent woman with a strong sense of social justice, Davison began to be interested in the women's suffrage movement in 1906. She was thirty-three and, for a woman of her time, exceptionally well educated. Having despaired of teaching in schools, she was trapped by her lack of family money into following one of the few occupations open to her: that of a live-in governess. For Davison, it likely meant intellectual, and social, suffocation. She was at this time, if we wish to picture her, in her prime. Sylvia Pankhurst described her appearance as 'tall and slender, with unusually long arms, a small narrow head and red hair. Her illusive, whimsical green eyes and thin, half-smiling mouth, bore often the mocking expression of the Mona Lisa.'

The women's suffrage message was spreading across the land and the movement received increasing attention in the press, not least due to the high-profile acts of suffragists such as Christabel Pankhurst. Prompted by curiosity, in 1906 Davison is thought to have attended a London rally hosted by the Women's Social and Political Union (WSPU), at which Emmeline and Christabel Pankhurst, the leaders of the Union, were speaking. She was sold on the organisation's mission – first and foremost, winning the vote for women – and applied for membership immediately. At thirty-four years old, she officially joined the WSPU as a 'foot soldier' among their ranks.

Even at this early juncture, Davison chose participation in one of the more militant suffrage groups that had developed. Splits in the movement had meant several organisations had sprung up. The WSPU, founded just three years earlier, was a militant breakaway group from the National Union of Women's Suffrage Societies (NUWSS), a long-established grassroots organisation that had come out of 1860s Manchester, which promoted only peaceful means of calling for constitutional change. The NUWSS, led by suffragist

Millicent Fawcett, actively distanced themselves from their former colleagues, the militant upstarts of the WSPU.

Davison was drawn to militancy from the start, believing that direct action was the most impactful way of breaking through the inertia of the male politicians. The early aims of the WSPU involved recruiting working-class women into the cause for female emancipation and this too would likely have appealed to Davison. The daughter of a poor house-keeper whose status had risen only to fall back into difficulty again in widowhood, she retained a deep sympathy for the plight of working-class women, and threw herself into social work where she could. Later, for instance, as she came to spend more time in London, she allied herself closely with the Workers' Educational Association, a federation of volun-tary groups convened to extend the opportunities in higher education to a wider, working-class audience. She would later become an executive of the Marylebone branch of the association.

By 1906, the WSPU was in the process of stepping up its new campaign of militancy, moving away from traditional techniques of political pressure, such as organising depu-tations and drafting petitions, towards active operations and violent acts. The Union moved its headquarters from Manchester to London to be closer to the seat of power and so that its activities would be more visible to the gen-eral public. Their new metropolitan location off the Strand, at 4 Clement's Inn, also afforded the group the chance to convene bigger events and attract greater numbers of people and publicity. The prospect of protests around Parliament, where WSPU suffragists had threatened to chain themselves to the railings outside the House of Commons, forced the government to pay attention to the movement. The WSPU proceeded slowly at first, but 1906 became the first year of significant civil uprising in the name of the women's movement.

In June, around thirty suffragists protested outside the house of Herbert Asquith, then Chancellor of the Exchequer in the Liberal government. The women, some of them clutching babies to their breasts, clashed violently with the police. A striking account of the arrest of one of their number remains in police records: 'A policeman proceeded to strike her with his fist, and she accordingly slapped his face. The policeman came forward and pinioned her, taking her by the throat and forcing her backwards so that she became blue in the face. With that she kicked the policeman's shins, and was arrested.' Excessive force, aggression, and even casual sexual assault by police against the suffragists were to become running themes.

In October, WSPU members began protesting outside the House of Commons. They were arrested and imprisoned. The Union also started a campaign of raucously protesting against candidates resistant to their cause at by-elections. These signs of a new stridency, marked by an escalation in the strategy of suffragists, were not the first militant acts that had been performed in the name of feminism. Firebrand activists had acted in stand-alone incidents on numerous occasions in the preceding decades. Dora Montefiore was one such high-profile activist. Born in Surrey, the daughter of an engineer who was one of the forces behind the 1951 Great Exhibition, Dora married an Australian merchant called George Montefiore. After he died at sea in 1889, however, she discovered that the law as it stood meant she had no automatic legal right to be her own children's guardian. Outraged, she was immediately to became a leader in the struggle for women's rights.

Montefiore joined, and became active in, Millicent Fawcett's National Union of Suffrage Societies, and was a keen advocate of non-payment of taxes as a legitimate weapon in the cause of winning the vote. In 1906, in a famous imitation of the Boston Tea Party, she declared: 'Taxation without representation is tyranny', and declined to hand over any money to the state. Bailiffs besieged her house in Hammersmith for six weeks, demanding her furniture and any other sellable possessions in lieu of unpaid taxes. Crowds gathered around her house in support, and she, in turn, addressed them from the upper windows. In the end, the bailiffs won the immediate struggle, her effects being sold off. However, Montefiore won the larger victory and she was adopted as an early heroine in the cause. She later became a communist activist, representing Australian communists at a convention in Moscow at the age of seventy-three. A resilient, hardy woman, she died in Sussex aged eighty-two.

While the vocal suffragists of the WSPU threw themselves into planning and executing militant acts, most self-described suffragists held fast to the more temperate tactics of the NUWSS, instead preferring to sign petitions and organise peaceful marches. Meanwhile many men and women remained on the sidelines of the women's suffrage debate altogether. The militancy of the WSPU was disdained by much of the population and the mainstream press. With a sneer, the *Daily Mail* christened the suffragist adherents of the WSPU's creed, 'suffragettes', and poured scorn on their 'unwomanly' tactics. The suffragists' response, an indication of how adroit they were becoming in their campaigning, was to adopt the intended insult 'suffragette' and repurpose it as a label of pride.[vii]

Parliament was similarly divided in its view of women's suffrage. There were plenty of die-hard opponents of any extension of the franchise, while some believed more working men should get a ballot, but a significant minority of MPs were sympathetic towards the notion of handing women the vote. However, none, whatever their opinion, could now ignore the movement, so vociferous was the multi-faceted campaign. It was a year of political upheaval in other ways too: in February came a general election. The Liberal Party won a landslide victory, which buoyed the spirits of suffragettes who knew the Liberals' leader, Henry Campbell-Bannerman, to be a supporter of women's suffrage, as were many of his MPs. Suffragette spirits rose, but it was to be the first of many times in the next eight years

---

vii   Initially the female activists pronounced the word 'suffragette' with a hard 'g' as a tongue-in-check reference to their slogan 'Get The Vote!'

when their hopes were raised only to be swiftly deflated as politicians' promises collapsed.

Davison was still working as a governess at this point, but was beginning to see more of the world. Postcards sent to family members between 1903 and 1908 revealed that during this period she was resident in the household of Sir Francis Layland-Barratt, the Liberal MP for Torquay. He owned houses in Cadogan Square in London, Cromer in Norfolk and Torquay in Devon. Working for the illustrious family, she also travelled with the three children to Genoa and Florence in 1905.[5]

However, apart from the occasional journey to London, Davison was starved of the companionship, erudite or otherwise, of her peers and colleagues at the WSPU for whom she felt increasing affinity. As a resident governess, she occupied a unique position within the households of the families who employed her – higher in rank than the servants, but not elevated enough to socialise or dine with the family. She was caught, then, on the mezzanine floor of Edwardian life; neither up, nor down. For two years from 1906 she was a member of the WSPU, but felt unable to commit wholly to its cause. Her job tutoring the children of wealthy, provincial families meant she was likely forced to keep her suffragette sympathies low-key, if not a secret. She could not risk the disapproval of the parents of her wards. To add to this claustrophobia, Davison was stuck in the country without like-minded friends with whom to share ideas and debate. It was a lonely and isolating life.

Professional opportunities for women were strictly limited at the turn of the twentieth century. In 1900, while 1.74 million women served as domestic help, there were only 212 female doctors and a sole pair of female architects, individuals who were looked upon as, at best, exceptions to the all-male rules, and more generally, as subversive oddities. Many pro-suffrage newspapers lamented the lack of opportunity for women like Davison after her death. The *Daily Herald* noted: 'In a normal nation, Miss Davison's life might have gone on from distinction to distinction, a record of fine achievement throughout. In the Britain that murders mind, [and] thwarts and degrades so much brave humanity, it was largely one of protest culminating in martyrdom.'

As her interest and involvement in the cause began to grow, the WSPU suffered a major split. The increasingly dictatorial tone taken by Emmeline Pankhurst and her daughters sparked a backlash among other senior figures in 1907. Charlotte Despard and several colleagues wanted to implement a committee structure to preside over decision-making. They proposed introducing elections for seats on an executive committee to take place at an annual meeting. Emmeline Pankhurst reacted furiously to the bureaucratic ideas, arguing that they would distract attention from the cause, and cancelled the proposed meeting. She and Christabel felt that 'complete unity in the ranks' was required to progress the cause.[6]

The row between Emmeline and Charlotte Despard was summed up by the WSPU's principal donor Emmeline

Pethick-Lawrence: 'These two notable women presented a great contrast, the one aflame with a single idea that had taken complete possession of her, the other upheld by a principle that had actuated a long life spent in the service of the people.'[7] Despard and her colleagues resigned. The split made front page news in the *Daily Mirror*.[viii]

Despite its internal struggles, the WSPU's audacity continued to increase throughout that year and the Union's suffragettes reached a turning point in 1908. In January, the first suffragettes chained themselves to the railings of 10 Downing Street. Three months later, however, the movement suffered a setback that would prove grave. Henry Campbell-Bannerman was forced to resign as prime minister on the grounds of ill health. His successor, Herbert Henry Asquith, was known to be against women's suffrage and had vocally scorned the idea since the 1880s. He had since learnt to present himself a little more ambiguously on the issue, but his arrival at 10 Downing Street was a great blow to the suffragettes' hopes of political reform. Although publicly Asquith agreed that his personal judgment should not overshadow the consensus of the House of Commons, he went on to employ delaying tactics to avoid a vote on the matter. Later during his premiership, in 1910, 1911 and 1912, three Conciliation bills were brought forth

---

viii   This was not the only major split in the WSPU. In 1912 it split again, after Emmeline Pethick-Lawrence and her husband Frederick, a wealthy couple who had financed the movement from its early days, clashed with Mrs Pankhurst and her daughters. The former pair were concerned about the increasing militancy of the movement and feared it could lead to activists dying. The Pankhursts refused to scale down the militancy and the Pethick-Lawrences were purged.

which would have extended the right to vote in parliamentary elections to a limited number of property-owning women, but Asquith starved the bills of parliamentary debating time and therefore they floundered. Optimists might have thought Asquith was merely taking his time, but increasingly the suffragettes realised he was beguiling them.

The members of the WSPU, as well as those from other suffrage groups, were outraged. They saw an inherent connection between liberalism and feminism and had counted on cooperation from the Liberal government, who had promised general reform in their election manifesto. When it became clear that Asquith and his ministers were not going to support them, their disappointment was crushing – they saw an ideological betrayal in the Liberal government's refusal to act.

It was against this background that Davison began to devote an increasing amount of her time to the cause. She became an officer in the WSPU and in June 1908 was given the role of chief steward at a show of protest in Hyde Park. It was the first of many such rallies hosted by the Union. The demonstration, held on 21 June 1908, was a carefully orchestrated affair: seven battalions of women marching from seven different starting points and converging in Hyde Park for a large meeting. The next day, *The Times* reported that the crowd there numbered an astonishing half a million people, and by no means all of them were women.

Emily was positioned as steward at Great Central Station, now Marylebone Station, the terminus for trains arriving from Manchester, Sheffield, Nottingham and Leicester. She and her comrades stood by to greet protesters travelling from these cities and over sixty other provincial towns. Emily welcomed the hordes, pointing them in the direction of marshals stationed on the streets to begin marching to Hyde Park. A contemporary wrote: 'She was glad and happy in the task; one who shared it testifies to her brightness and energy, and to her keen regret that she was obliged to return to her pupils before the whole work of the day was done.'

There were banners and brass bands, and some twenty platforms were erected around the park for dozens – possibly as many as eighty – different speakers. The day was known as 'Women's Sunday', and the throng attending even had special tickets carrying the legend 'Votes For Women' printed in the suffragette colours of purple for liberty and dignity, white for purity and green for hope. The day ended with the passing by acclamation of a resolution stating: 'This meeting calls upon the Government to grant votes to women without delay.' Delay, however, was precisely what lay in store.

Emily applied herself to her new role in the Union with enthusiasm, and it is easy to imagine how the energy and excitement surrounding the cause cast a long shadow over her duties as a governess. The tension between her job and her commitment to the suffrage cause was growing. Becoming increasingly addicted to the thrill of the struggle, Emily yearned to abandon the life of teaching and become a full-time campaigner. It would be another year before she would take the leap from secure employment to unpaid activism, but she did in the meantime leave the teaching post she had held for the past six years and moved to tutor another family. The reason for the change is not known, but her increasing involvement with the WSPU may well have become an issue for her former employer.

In addition to Davison's private disgruntlement with her occupation, she was unhappy being stuck in the middle of countryside far from the metropolitan-based WSPU. She had grown up in the chaotic, bustling atmosphere of the capital and she longed to be back in her hometown. Although she enjoyed spells in the rugged hills of Northumberland with her mother later in life, her heart lay in London, to which she wrote an undated paean:

> Oh, London! How I feel thy magic spell
> Now I have left thee, and amid the woods
> Sit lonely. Here I know I love thee well,
> Conscious of all the glamour of thy moods.
> But it is otherwise amid thy bounds!
> Thou art an ocean of humanity!
> Embarked on which I lose my soul in sounds
> That thunder in mine ear. The vanity
> And ceaseless struggle stifle doubt and fear
> Until I cry, bemused by the strife,
> 'The centre of the universe is here!
> This is the hub, the very fount of life.'

Although she may have shared with friends her desire to break free from tutoring and commit herself fully to the suffragette cause, to the rest of the world she gave no sign of this. Her former headmistress, referring to the meetings between the two, later wrote:

> I never heard her complain or express anxiety about her own future or that of her mother. I never heard her utter a word against anyone under whom or with whom she worked, and no one ever had less thought of adopting a 'misunderstood' pose, or the role of the neglected govern-ess. On the contrary, she spoke of her affection for her pupils and of the kindness she received from their parents.

In 1909 Davison finally gave up teaching for good. It is likely that she could no longer continue in post while immersing herself in the WSPU. She was not a moderate or half-hearted individual; her singularity of purpose and obsessive nature would not allow her to devote less than her entire attention to the cause in which she had come to believe in so deeply.

Nonetheless, it was a brave move – the 36-year-old had no private income with which to support herself, and her mother, struggling herself to make ends meet, was also unable to fund her existence. She was, however, called to give herself wholly to the women's suffrage movement. With an equanimity that became characteristic of her demeanour throughout her militant years, she left her job and moved to London.

CHAPTER 4

THE BEGINNINGS OF MILITANCY
MARCH–OCTOBER 1909

D avison's prominence in the WSPU grew as her willingness to carry out militant acts became increasingly apparent to the leadership. After dedicating herself to the movement full time she was swiftly promoted from backroom administrative duties and stewarding at meetings to an activist trusted with secret missions plotted by the leadership.

In March 1909, a year after joining the organisation, she took her first step towards what would become an intense career of militancy, enjoying her first direct actions in the name of women's suffrage, as well as her first brush with the law. As part of a deputation to Asquith in March, she boldly attempted to thrust a petition into the Prime Minister's hands and was swiftly arrested. Unafraid to sully a clean legal record and begin a criminal one, she refused to give an undertaking to cease attendance at all such deputations in future – an offer extended to her in lieu of prosecution on the basis of her previous good character.

Ten days after the incident she was sentenced in court to one month in prison. Her self-sacrifice in undergoing a prison sentence was acknowledged in the suffragette press. In the paper *Votes for Women*, she was described on 2 April as playing a fundamental role in the London campaign and as being a valued member of the Union.

In June she described her own commitment to the cause in the same newspaper, explaining, 'Through my humble work in this noblest of all causes, I have come into a fullness of joy and an interest in living which I never experienced.'[8]

A matter of months later, Emily was arrested again, this time for obstruction. On 30 July, she violently attempted to barge into the Edinburgh Castle, a music hall and gin palace in Limehouse, east London, where the Chancellor of the Exchequer was giving a speech. In his address, David Lloyd George detailed the government's revolutionary 'People's Budget', which was the first in the country's history to aim to redistribute wealth. Apart from a pair of women on the platform, all other female attendees were forbidden in the hall; it was men alone who were permitted to decide, or even hear about, the country's finances. This state of affairs was intolerable to the suffragettes gathered outside and they attempted to force their way in. Those who managed to break into the hall were leapt upon by stewards, but not before they had succeeded in disrupting the meeting and causing chaos.

The din inside the hall was doubled by the sounds of the gathered throng of women shouting outside.

Davison herself wrote: 'I was busy haranguing the crowd when the police came up and arrested me.' The repeat offence saw her sentence doubled to two months. She and her newfound friend, fellow suffragette Mary Leigh, received the longest sentences; most of their comrades were sentenced to two weeks in prison. Once they were jailed, the group demanded to find out their prisoner status. They were hoping to be classified as first-class prisoners, a privilege afforded to all men imprisoned for political crimes. The women claimed they were entitled to the same status. The governor dashed their hopes, however, and a struggle broke out. Each suffragette was manhandled to her cell. Emily was furious. She wrote to a friend:

When I was shut in the cell I at once smashed seventeen panes of glass. Please, if you are asked why we did this, say, because we object to the fact that the windows can never be opened, and the ventilation is bad.

They forcibly undressed me and left me sitting in a prison chemise. I sang the second verse of 'God Save the King,' with 'Confound their politics' in it! The doctor came in to sound me, and I refused to be sounded [examined with a stethoscope]. Then I was dressed in prison clothes and taken into one of the worst cells, very dark, with double doors.

Resorting to the bedtime ritual of her girlhood, she sang hymns to keep her spirits up – and to remind prison officers that she was there, defiant, and in no mood to compromise or relent. She later wrote of this stint in Holloway: 'In the dark punishment cell, to my delight, I found on my wall Mrs. Dove-Willcox's name,[ix] and "Dum spiro spero".[x] I added mine and "Rebellion against tyrants is obedience to God."'[xi] The slogan had by this time become her personal motto, and the creed upon which she acted.

Davison then decided to follow the practice pioneered a month earlier by fellow suffragette Marion Wallace-Dunlop: the hunger strike. Scottish-born Wallace-Dunlop was the artist daughter of a senior figure in the Indian civil service. In the summer of 1908, she had been convicted for throwing stones at the windows of 10 Downing Street. Her allies insisted she had used pebbles, while the newspapers described her missiles as rocks. A year later, on 25 June 1909, she went to St Stephen's Hall in the House of Commons and took out a rubber stamp charged with indelible ink. With this, she marked the stonework of the building with a women's rights slogan. She was found guilty of wilful damage to the tune of 10 shillings, at that time the price of a pound of meat, but she refused to pay the fine and so was sent to Holloway Prison

---

ix   Lillian Dove-Willcox was a member of Emmeline Pankhurst's personal bodyguard. The suffragette had been arrested in 1909 after lobbying for the WSPU outside the House of Commons. Widowed the year before, she went on to open up her home for convalescing hunger-strikers.

x   'While I breathe, I hope'.

xi   Alongside graffiti, many incarcerated suffragettes managed to communicate with each other, and the outside world, by smuggling messages scribbled on lavatory paper.

for a month. There she expected to be granted political status, petitioning the governor of the prison with the words:

> I claim the right recognised by all civilised nations that a person imprisoned for a political offence should have first-division treatment; and as a matter of principle, not only for my own sake but for the sake of others who may come after me, I am now refusing all food until this matter is settled to my satisfaction.

Her petition was spurned, and so she refused to eat, thus starting the infamous hunger strikes that marked the suffrage campaign throughout subsequent years. Wallace-Dunlop held to her fast for ninety-one hours before the authorities, fearing a death on their hands, released her. Inspiring legions of suffragettes thereafter, she gave a speech that year which encapsulated the philosophy of the women's suffrage movement:

> Women have grown to realise their responsibility not only as individuals but also as members of a great community … they have in fact at last recognised that they are part and parcel of what we may call the public conscience.

Davison was similarly denied the right to be treated as a political prisoner and so she followed suit in staging a hunger strike. It was to be the first of many which would weaken and waste away her tall, lithe body. In this instance, the strike tactic was successful and after an arduous five-day fast, she was released. She wrote to a friend: 'I fasted 124 hours, and was then released. I lost 1 ½ stone and much flesh. I felt very weak at first, but I am pulling up rapidly now. My mother is making me feed up hard, and I am being very lazy.' She then added, with characteristic nonchalance: 'What did you think of me? I suppose you are in Switzerland now? Do send me some picture postcards ... Please write soon, To your Loving and rebellious friend, Emelye.'

Christabel Pankhurst was overjoyed at the results of the tactic adopted by Wallace-Dunlop and then Davison. She wrote, in a statement that would prove to be short-sighted in the wake of the authorities' retaliation:

> We are feeling proud at having destroyed the Government's weapon of coercion. They will never in future be able to keep us in prison more than a few days, for we have now learnt to use our power to starve ourselves out of prison, and this power we shall use – unless of course the Government prefer to let us die.

The hunger strike initially proved a remarkably effective political tactic for the suffragettes, ensuring their release from prison and generating publicity for the cause. The suffragettes' hunger striking also served to convey a deeper cultural message to patriarchal British society. It was, as Jane Marcus, a professor of feminist literature, asserts, a method by which the British woman could refuse the role foisted upon her by society of mother and nurturer of the country. The Edwardian male public was shocked and appalled by the thought of respectable women reduced to an emaciated state. Ideals central to their notion of femininity – gentility, dependence, weakness of mind and body – were shattered by this rebellious practice. Hunger striking may have made women's bodies frail, but it demonstrated their collective strength, iron-fast resolve and seriousness of intention.

A sense of camaraderie was crucial in maintaining a prolonged fast. In all the hunger strikes Davison undertook, she complained of her anxiety at being kept away from her comrades in solitary confinement, unable to check if they were bearing up and keeping strong, and no doubt eager for a morale boost herself. In a canny move, the WSPU established an honours system to recognise and revere the heroines in their midst who undertook fasts. 'Holloway' brooches were designed by the Union as medals of fortitude. Serving as an acknowledgement of the courage of those women who willingly accepted jail sentences and undertook hunger strikes, they also encouraged other activists to step up and win praise. Sylvia Pankhurst's design for the brooches, which featured the House of Commons portcullis intercepted by a prison arrow, was a mocking symbol of the second-class status of suffragette prisoners.

Davison took great strength from her religious conviction in the righteousness of her actions. She described on more than one occasion the calling from God she felt to carry out the duties of militant suffragism. Over time she developed an obsession with Joan of Arc, self-consciously adopting the attitudes of the iconic female martyr. Her motto – 'Rebellion against tyrants is obedience to God', a saying that was linked to United States Founding Fathers Benjamin Franklin and Thomas Jefferson – was also associated at the time with the older mythology surrounding the Maid of Orléans.

One suffragette comrade confirmed Davison's open religious devotion: 'She always said very long prayers and her Bible was always by her bedside.' Another childhood friend said of her faith:

> That she was heart and soul in the movement no one could doubt, or that she looked upon her share in it as a special work to which she had been called ... I regretted the line she took ... but I was convinced that she believed herself to be obeying a direct call.

Davison herself reportedly told her mother: 'I never do any of the things [acts of militancy] except under the [divine] Influence.' In two essays that she later wrote, 'The Real Christianity' and 'The Price of Liberty', she imagined herself specially chosen for the responsibility and called by God to fight for the cause. The religious conviction fuelling her actions, no matter if they endangered or harmed others, only grew.

Ravaged and emotionally drained from her first fast, she spent August of 1909 at home with her mother in Long-horsley. From this time onwards, the cycle of prison sentence and hunger strike, followed by rest and recuperation at her mother's house, became routine for Davison. She would never rest long, allowing herself only enough time to regain some strength to commit further militant acts. By September 1909, Emily was back in the fray and had graduated to more provocative vandalism. On 4 September she was sentenced for throwing rocks at the windows of a meeting of the Liberals in White City, Manchester, during a Budget demonstration. She and four comrades had eluded the police and broken panes of glass in the Concert Hall with iron balls nicknamed 'bombs'.[9] News of refined and well-educated women hurling rocks scandalised Edwardian society. 'Lunatics or criminals' screeched contemporary commentators.

The courts took a dim view of her behaviour. There was little chance of Davison and colleagues merely being bound over to keep the peace or told to go away and take up a calming hobby such as embroidery. At her sentencing, Davison was offered two options of punishment for the offence: either to pay a fine of £5 and 4 shillings for damage or to serve a sentence of two months in prison. Without hesitation she plumped for the latter and was carted off to HMP Strangeways in Manchester. Once again she and her fellow comrades protested their treatment and the refusal of the prison authorities to grant them political prisoner status, and undertook hunger strike. The prison guards, far from showing sympathy for the plight of the women resorting to such desperate means, resolved to treat them all the more brutally. They roughly handcuffed the suffragettes, jostled them, and even manhandled one of their number into a straitjacket. It was the beginning of a new tactic on the part of the authorities: to try to declare hunger-striking suffragettes clinically insane. The group would not capitulate, however, and after two days of imprisonment and hunger strike, they were released on 8 September – angry but triumphant. Although perturbed by the new, sterner methods of the authorities, Davison's resolve was stiffened by the heroic welcome she received upon returning home after her prison stint. The *Morpeth Herald* recounted:

Headed by a Brass Band, the … ladies and others drove in a brake to the railway station to await Miss Davison's arrival. Upon two of the banners displayed were the words, 'Welcome Northumberland hunger-striker' and 'Votes for Women.' On her arrival Miss Davison was escorted to a carriage drawn by two horses, and she 'drove in state,' followed by a brake load of Suffragists, the band leading the procession to the Market Place. There a large crowd of people assembled.[10]

She wasted little time in plotting her next headline-grabbing act. On the evening of 8 October, twelve senior suffragettes assembled in secret to plan a protest against Lloyd George, the Chancellor, who was scheduled to give a speech in Newcastle the following day. Davison decided to work together with fellow suffragette Lady Constance 'Con' Lytton, daughter of the first Earl of Lytton, Viceroy of India, and the highest-born senior figure in the suffragette movement.

Lytton had been refused permission by her mother to marry the man she loved because he was deemed socially inferior. Thereafter she declined to contemplate marriage again and threw herself headlong into the women's suffrage movement.

This was to be the first in a series of collaborations between the aristocrat and the daughter of a former housekeeper. Bringing women from different backgrounds together was a key effect of the movement, which encouraged many unlikely friendships. These opportunities for intermingling were rare in Edwardian Britain, but Davison's own circle of comrades shows that the movement straddled the class divide – her friends hailed from across the socio-economic spectrum, with some belonging to wealthy landed families and others, like her close friend Mary Leigh, coming from working-class backgrounds.

Davison and Lytton cemented their friendship on that first mission. They carefully plotted their strategy and carried it out to good effect. As Saturday afternoon came around, the pair dawdled inconspicuously outside the offices of the Newcastle Breweries, anxiously waiting. It was the closest they could advance to the central square in front of the theatre, which was barricaded off by legions of policemen. Lloyd George was driven to the theatre via backstreets in the car of his friend, Sir Walter Runciman, a shipping magnate with Liberal leanings. After Lloyd George was safely deposited at the theatre, Runciman proceeded to St George's Hall. As his vehicle passed the breweries headquarters, Davison and Lytton leapt forward from the shadows. Looking 'wild' and 'excited', as the following day's papers would describe her, Lytton launched a stone at the car. It missed its target. Before Davison could follow suit, they were pounced upon by nearby policemen and arrested. The cloth wrapped around the prepared missiles were scrawled with Davison's motto, followed by the suffragette slogan:

> To Lloyd George. Rebellion against tyrants is obedience
> to god. Deeds not words

The two women, along with nine comrades, were dragged off to Central Police Station. Colmore, Davison's contemporary biographer, offered an impassioned apologia for the suffragettes' stone-throwing that day. The missiles were destined strictly for the wheels of the passing car, she insisted, and were emphatically not meant to hit its occupants. It is an implausible argument, because the likeliest outcome of a sizeable object hitting the spoked wheels of a car would have been for it to range off the road. All possible outcomes from the stunt risked injury to their targets. There was, in this incident, and others – such as the growing practice of setting fire to sports pavilions and other edifices at night – a new recklessness to the suffragettes' activism. It was leapt upon by critics.

A fierce debate over the tactics used by the militant suffrage movement still rages today, and no individual sparks more divisive opinion than Emily Wilding Davison. Some feminists and historians still attempt to mount the defence that her intention was never to allow harm to anyone apart from herself. It is an overly generous interpretation. Davison's involvement in arson attacks and her final act at the Derby undeniably put people at risk of fatal injury. The attack on Lloyd George's car marked a turning point in her militancy, which began to scale up as her frustration at the government's inertia grew. The religious dimension of her fervour rendered her a true insurgent, and she felt emboldened by the divine dispensation she believed was granted to her cause.

CHAPTER 5

AN INCIDENT IN PRISON
OCTOBER 1909–1910

T he gaggle of suffragettes involved in the Newcastle stone-throwing incident appeared at the police court with six others the following Monday, after two days spent in the cells. Lady Constance Lytton was charged with assaulting Sir Walter Runciman. She received a four-week prison sentence, but was released after a two-and-a-half-day hunger strike on the grounds of pre-existing ill health. To expose and protest the preferential treatment she believed she had received, the next time she was arrested she sought to disguise her social status by adopting the pose of a worker and the pseudonym 'Jane Warton'. The ruse worked to devastating effect, leading to rough handling that permanently damaged her fragile health. She was jailed four times in all and, in the wake of her hunger strikes and force-feeding, eventually had a heart attack at the age of forty-one. She later died aged fifty-four.

Mary Leigh, the former schoolteacher and dedicated colleague of Davison's who, in later years, would travel to Northumberland to tend her grave on the anniversary of her death, had earlier been refused bail. She was sentenced to a month's imprisonment. Davison, accused of the lesser charge of attempted assault, was released.

Just over a fortnight later, in October 1909, Runciman was speaking in Radcliffe, Greater Manchester (then a part of Lancashire) at a Budget meeting, from which women were excluded. Only women accompanied by men were permitted to congregate around the venue; single women and groups of women were banned.[11] Colmore wrote of the suffragettes' response to these constraints: 'As no protest against the government's policy with regard to the franchise question could therefore be made within the meeting, a protest was made without, and Emily and three other women were arrested for breaking the windows of the post office and the Liberal club.' For her efforts, Davison was lauded in the WSPU as 'one of the most devoted voluntary workers in the Union, and has given up her whole life for the cause'.

The stones thrown were said to have been wrapped in messages to Runciman, including the slogan: 'He who would be free must strike the first blow.' In court Davison was reported to have admitted the charge, but insisted the action had been necessary in order to show the suffragettes' seriousness of intent. She said: 'As a woman taxpayer, we demand that the government give justice to women by granting them the vote on the same terms as men.'[12]

On 20 October, before she was sentenced and thrown into prison once again, she made a will and left all her belongings to her mother. She knew the dangers that lay ahead. Because, although she had already endured hunger strikes, this would be the first time she would experience the horror of force-feeding. It was a policy to which the government, humiliated at the ingenuity of the suffragettes, had resorted since her last stint in jail. The incarcerated suffragettes had adopted the hunger strike in Bury Police Court and continued it once inside Strangeways Prison. To the surprise of Davison and her fellow inmates, the authorities did not back down and release them, as they had before. It came as a shock to Davison that she would face the horrors of force-feeding.

She would likely have heard first-hand the testimonies of her friend Mary Leigh, who had been subjected to the practice the month before in Winson Green Prison in Birmingham. She had written about the ordeal and had passed her account to the WSPU so that they were able to get it published in a pamphlet while she was still in prison. Leigh said:

I was then surrounded and forced back onto the chair, which was tilted backward. There were about ten persons around me. The doctor then forced my mouth so as to form a pouch, and held me while one of the wardresses poured some liquid from a spoon; it was milk and brandy. After giving me what he thought was sufficient, he sprinkled me with eau de cologne, and wardresses then escorted me to another cell on the first floor, where I remained two days.

On Saturday afternoon the wardresses forced me onto the bed and the two doctors came in with them. While I was held down a nasal tube was inserted. It is two yards long, with a funnel at the end; there is a glass junction in the middle to see if the liquid is passing. The end is put up the right and left nostril on alternate days. Great pain is experienced during the process, both mental and physical.

One doctor inserted the end up my nostril while I was held down by the wardresses, during which process they must have seen my pain, for the other doctor interfered (the matron and two of the wardresses were in tears), and they stopped and resorted to feeding me by the spoon, as in the morning. More eau de cologne was used. The food was milk. I was then put to bed in the cell, which is a punishment cell on the first floor. The doctor felt my pulse and asked me to take food each time, but I refused...

The sensation is most painful – the drums of the ears seem to be bursting and there is a horrible pain in the throat and the breast. The tube is pushed down 20 inches. I am on the bed pinned down by wardresses, one doctor holds the funnel end, and the other doctor forces the other end up the nostrils. The one holding the funnel end pours the liquid down – about a pint of milk ... egg and milk is sometimes used.[13]

Davison was locked up in a solitary cell upon her arrival at the Manchester Prison and was subject to force-feeding within twenty-four hours.

Towards evening, two doctors, a handful of wardresses, and the prison matron entered her cell and the horror unfolded. She detailed her experience in a letter to an unnamed friend:

The doctor said 'I am going to feed you by force.' The scene, which followed, will haunt me with its horror all my life, and is almost indescribable. While they held me flat, the elder doctor tried all round my mouth with a steel gag to find an opening. On the right side of my mouth two teeth are missing; this gap he found, pushed in the horrid instrument, and prised open my mouth to its widest extent. Then a wardress poured liquid down my throat out of a tin enamelled cup. What it was I cannot say, but there was some medicament, which was foul to the last degree. As I would not swallow the stuff and jerked it out with my tongue, the doctor pinched my nose and somehow gripped my tongue with the gag. The torture was barbaric.

Emily's description of the barbaric practice as 'torture' is apt. The practice was agonisingly painful, frightening and humiliating. The suffragettes were well aware of the perils of the practice; Davison and some of her comrades – otherwise young, healthy women – who resolved to endure forcible feeding wrote wills around this time, in the knowledge that the practice entailed a very real risk of death.

Overall, historian Martin Pugh estimates that 241 suffragettes undertook hunger strike, and, of that number, 130 were
forcibly fed. Women emerged from jail with 'bruises, bleeding
noses, injured mouths and throats, damaged teeth, pulled-out
hair, bloodshot eyes, high blood pressure, and dehydration'.

The testimony of Constance Lytton recalls similar cruelty
on the part of the prison team and horrifying distress:

Two of the women (wardresses) took hold of my arms, one
held my head and one my feet. One wardress helped to
pour the food. The doctor leant on my knees as he stooped
over my chest to get at my mouth. I shut my mouth and
clenched my teeth. The sense of being overpowered by
more force than I could possibly resist was complete, but
I resisted nothing except with my mouth. The doctor offered me the choice of a wooden or steel gag; he explained
that the steel gag would hurt and the wooden one would
not, and he urged me not to force him to use the steel one.
But I did not speak nor open my mouth, so after playing
about for a moment or two with the wooden one he finally
had recourse to the steel.

The pain of it was intense; he got the gag between my
teeth, when he proceeded to turn it much more than necessary until my jaws were fastened wide apart, far more
than they could go naturally. Then he put down my throat
a tube, which seemed to me much too wide and was something like four feet long. The irritation of the tube was
excessive. I choked the moment it touched my throat until

it had gone down. Then the food was poured in quickly; it made me sick a few seconds after it was down and the action of the sickness made my body and legs double up, but the wardresses instantly pressed back my head and the doctor leant on my knees. The horror of it was more than I can describe. I had been sick over my hair, all over the wall near my bed, and my clothes seemed saturated with vomit. The wardresses told me that they could not get a change [of clothes] as it was too late, the office was shut.

One suffragette, Lilian Lenton, was pushed to the brink of death in 1913 after a bungled attempt at force-feeding meant food was poured into her lung, instead of her stomach, and caused a severe case of septic pneumonia. Lenton, the daughter of a Leicester carpenter, had trained to be a dancer, but, at twenty-one, joined the WSPU, and embarked on a career of window smashing and arson. The incident which led to her imprisonment and near-fatal brush with force-feeding came in February 1913, when she was arrested for setting fire to the Tea House at Kew Gardens. She was sent to Holloway Prison. The rough and careless incident of force-feeding received a great deal of publicity and was widely condemned.

A prominent surgeon, Victor Horsley, wrote to *The Times*:

The Home Secretary's attempted denial that Miss Lenton was nearly killed by the forcible feeding is worthless ... she was tied into a chair and her head dragged backward across the back of the chair by her hair. The tube was forced through the nose twice … after the second introduction when the food was poured in, it caused violent choking.

Lenton recovered and was undeterred from avoiding arrest or eschewing hunger strike in the aftermath of the incident. She was repeatedly arrested for arson until the First World War brought about a cessation in suffragette militancy.

Mishaps concerning forcible feeding were relatively common. Mary Clark, Emmeline Pankhurst's sister, died on Christmas Day in 1910 just forty-eight hours after she had been released from Holloway Prison. She had suffered an embolism following force-feeding and was described in her obituary by Emmeline Pethick-Lawrence as 'the first woman martyr who has gone to death for this cause'.

The dangers of the practice were highlighted again in 1917 when Thomas Ashe, an Irish Republican prisoner, died from complications relating to being force-fed in Mountjoy Jail in Dublin. It took until 1975, when the World Medical Association passed the Declaration of Tokyo, for the practice to be banned, though not without complications and abuses since. In 1981 hunger strikes were used to devastating effect by IRA leaders, led by Bobby Sands, in the Northern Irish prison, HM Maze. Ten Republicans died before the strike was called off in October that year. Like the suffragettes before them, the prisoners had protested their classification as criminals rather than the 'special category' of political prisoners. Their hunger strikes marked the culmination of a five-year protest.

The forcible entry of instruments into an individual's body

during force-feeding was a violation tantamount to rape, some commentators have argued.[14] The penetration aspect of forcible feeding appears to have been the most traumatic for many suffragettes and was highlighted time and again in their testimonies.

The procedure involved several people holding down the subject by force, a doctor ramming rubber tubing down through the subject's throat – often through the more painful nasal route – and pouring a viscous mixture of liquidised food and medicine down into the tube. The practice was agonising for the subject, but also largely ineffective. In terms of nourishment, force-feeding provided very little, meaning that hunger-striking suffragettes were still released from prison in an emaciated state – the practice only prolonging their incarceration for a short period. In political terms, the horror of the treatment did not deter the women from hunger striking either. In all, it afforded little gain to the authorities.

Whether the male doctors who administered the treatment felt any shame is unclear, but it spoke to wider cultural issues in male-dominated Edwardian society. As academic Dr Joyce Kay concludes: 'That this could be condoned in a "civilised" state says much about the attitude of a society that was still essentially patriarchal.' Brutalised by the barbaric treatment of male staff in prison, a growing number of suffragettes began to feel that male politicians were apt targets for retaliation.

In November *The Suffragette* published an account by

Davison of the harsh practice alongside numerous other shocking testimonies from her comrades. A publicity campaign against the practice was launched, as suffragettes, doctors and even some politicians spoke out against the 'torture'. Davison did not accept such savage treatment lightly. In protest against her first experience of force-feeding on the Friday, she smashed the windows of her prison cell over the weekend. On the Monday, therefore, she was moved into an adjoining cell. Entering, she saw that this cell contained two plank beds, the bed belonging to this cell and the one they had taken from the cell she had been moved from. Characteristically quick-witted, she immediately calculated how these could be used to barricade the door.

Working speedily and quietly, Colmore recounts how:

She put the two beds lengthways one beyond the other across the floor of the cell. A space of about two feet remained between the second bed and the wall; the stool legs upwards, she filled it and the wedge not being quite firm, her two slippers and a hairbrush were jammed in to make it quite secure. On the only doubtful spot, the place where the two beds joined, she sat down, and, having piled up the table and mattress to add to the weight, quietly waited.

The wardress came, and, finding the door stuck, demanded that Davison open it. Sitting tight, with rigid determination, she smiled and replied firmly: 'No.'

There she remained all afternoon, as a succession of prison officials came, and, alternately imploring and threatening her, demanded that she take down her barricade. They appealed to all manner of manoeuvres to prise open the door, but to no avail. Eventually the governor arrived, and a wardress ordered: 'Get off the planks!' She neither budged, nor uttered a word. The governor was infuriated by this defiance, and threatened her: 'Davison, if you don't get off those planks and open the door we shall turn the hose-pipe on you.' A ladder was leant against the outer wall, the window to her cell smashed and the nozzle of a hosepipe forced into the room. The prison authorities took their time, menacingly fixing the hosepipe into position, before offering her one more chance to back down. Once more, she declined.

So the icy assault began, and freezing water pounded over Davison's head as she held fast to her bed boards. Realising that the throbbing stream was not hitting their target, the prison wardens altered the course of the water so that it pelted her with full force. 'I had to hold on,' she later said, 'like grim death.' For fully fifteen minutes she held out against the icy jet, before the hose operator paused, and a prison warden, fearful of killing her, ordered: 'Stop! No more, no more.' Their savage attempt to break Davison's spirit and force her to disassemble her barricade had failed.

The prison authorities now had no alternative but to break down the sizeable, heavy door. If they did, however, and it fell, it would crush the prisoner beneath its weight. The men outside realised the risk; so did the woman within. Nonetheless the warders took a chance. They rammed the door and it gave way, missing Davison by a tiny margin. Water, six inches deep, rushed out of the room flooding the corridor. A prison warden darted in and, seizing Davison, growled at her: 'You ought to be horsewhipped for this.' She was pushed into her former cell, undressed, and rushed to the prison hospital covered in blankets. There she was given a warming bath and hot water bottle, while news of the hosepipe incident, and her steely response, spread. She was given no reprieve, however, and, shortly afterwards, was forcibly fed through the nose.

She was mentally and physically exhausted by the incident. She lay in bed for three days afterwards, until the prison wardens decided to force her to exercise, showing no mercy towards the weak prisoner. So limp and frail was her body, however, that the authorities changed their opinion and released her that afternoon.

Lady Constance Lytton, in her 1914 book *Prisons & Prisoners*, wrote that the hosepipe incident had brought Davison the closest she had yet come to death:

Soon after this Miss Davison was forcibly fed in Manchester Prison, and, on barricading her cell, the hose-pipe was played upon her from the window, a process of force that caused her infinite pain. She fainted, and it was many days before she recovered. She owed her life probably to being released from prison, and to the fact that she was a great swimmer, used to the shock of cold water and to withstanding its force.

As she walked through the prison gates to freedom, Davison was amazed to find that the hosepipe incident had filled the newspapers all over the country and had even been raised in Parliament. Once the news had broken, the outrage was such that thousands of protesters had gathered to demonstrate outside Strangeways Prison, with a crowd of 9,000 on the biggest day of protest.

The public outrage at her treatment refused to abate. The *Manchester Guardian* said in its leading article, which was reproduced by *Votes for Women*:

> There has shown itself of late a tendency to treat women who offend in this way especially in public meetings, with a certain degree of retaliatory violence, as though the fact that they are women were in itself an extreme aggravation of their offence and anything might be done to them. It is a sort of recrudescence of the sentiments which once found expression in the scold's bridle and the ducking-stool. Against this tendency it is the business of all responsible people to set themselves. We do not for a moment contend that women who break the law and commit wanton offenses against person or property are to expect to escape punishment on the ground of sex or of motive, but inasmuch as most or all of them are acting under a sense of public wrong it is all the more important in dealing with them to give no sort of ground for an added sense of personal wrong.[15]

Keir Hardie, the leader of the Labour Party, raised questions about the incident on the floor of the House of Commons. On 28 October 1909, he rose and asked:

I wish to ask the Home Secretary a question of which I have given him private notice, whether he can say by whose authority a fire-hose pipe was played on one of the women suffragettes in Strangeways Gaol, Manchester; whether the lady was at the time weak from want of food; whether the water was played upon her for about an hour; and what action he has taken to punish those responsible for author-ising and carrying out this assault upon a prisoner?

Home Secretary Herbert Gladstone merely replied: 'The newspaper statement is true.'

In addition, Philip Snowden, another Labour MP, took up Davison's cause and demanded that members of the Visiting Committee, whose task it was to ensure that prisoners were treated within the rules, should be sacked from their offices as Justices of the Peace. One man on that Committee, James Johnson, a Manchester city councillor, moved a resolution of protest stating that as a Justice of the Peace he refused to stand by the action of his colleagues. The general public, not always in agreement with militancy in the women's suffrage movement, in this instance sided firmly with the rebels and concurred that the treatment of Emily Wilding Davison had been an appalling abuse. Spurred on by public support, therefore, Davison decided to take the authorities responsi-ble for the hosepipe incident to court.

In January, she brought a charge against the local visiting justices of Strangeways in respect of the 'tact, care, humanity and firmness' with which they had treated her in blasting her with the icy water. The case was heard on 10 January, but met no immediate resolution, with the judge reserving judgment.

Gordon Havant, representing Davison, had told the court:

> My client is of considerable intellectual distinction and is a member of an association that has sought to maintain that a taxpayer ought not to be debarred from voting for a representative of the House of Commons. She pursued her policy of protest in prison and refused to put on prison uniform or to take food. This resulted in forcible feeding which was physically painful and extremely repulsive and degrading. Determined not to submit to it any longer she barricaded her door on 25 October 1909. Instead of taking the door off the hinges the defendants had the hosepipe turned on her. Consequently an assault and battery had been committed for which there was no justification. The result of the drenching was that she was afterwards kept confined to bed for a considerable time and was unable to resume her literary work.

Asked in court why she thought the hose had been turned on her, she answered: 'I would say to frighten me.'[16]

The representative of the defendants, the visiting justices at Strangeways Prison, countered:

> In recent times there had grown up a class of misdemeanants

who were disorderly and brawled in the streets and public places and did what the law called wilful damage and they were sent to prison for their offences. These women had traded on the weakness of their sex to avoid the consequences of their misconduct. The plaintiff entered the prison with the avowed intention of breaking every rule and this she did … She admitted in an article she wrote to the newspaper that if the door had fallen in she would have been crushed. The witnesses say that instead of being a punishment, the turning of the water was done entirely for the good of the plaintiff to remove her from the position where she would inevitably have been seriously hurt or perhaps killed, if the door had fallen upon her.

The governor of Strangeways also took to the stand. He said:

Many of the most depraved and violent classes of prisoner behaved splendidly in prison and their cells are a great credit to them but the insubordination on the part of these women, if it is not stamped out, will soon affect other classes of prisoners. The breaking of a cell door, which is fitted in an iron frame, has special locks and is a serious and expensive matter. I believe the officials were justified in taking every means of securing an entrance before they forced the door.

Judge Parry finally pronounced in Davison's favour on 19 January 1910. The suffragette was awarded a paltry 40 shillings (£2) for a 'technical breach of the rules on the part of the Strangeways authority'. Although a small concession, with only 'technical' fault conceded, it was a significant victory for the women's suffrage movement. The rules had been breached, and Davison had proved that.

In his summing up, the judge had turned his focus to Davison. He noted:

> The plaintiff's conduct in gaol was deliberately and for a set purpose directed towards the annoyance of those in charge of her. One might admit that this was not done merely from a desire to irritate but from a wider motive. The particular officials who have had to suffer from the plaintiff's conduct seem to have acted with every discretion and kindness … The plaintiff has had the satisfaction of bringing a lawsuit against the Justices for a momentary indiscretion and providing herself with 'copy' for a vivacious and entertaining account of the affair in the press [laughter] and advertising a cause which she and many others are greatly interested. Under the circumstances the damages should be nominal and I assess them at 40s.[17]

It would be far from the last time Davison appeared in court. In future, however, she would eschew legal representation and would speak for herself.

Despite the growing public unease surrounding the treatment of suffragettes in prison, many government figures stood resolutely by the authorities. In January 1910, a few months after the soaking of Emily and the breaking down of the cell door that could have killed her, Herbert Gladstone, Home Secretary in the Liberal government and son of former Prime Minister William Gladstone, wrote a letter of praise to the officials at Strangeways Prison. Part of it read:

> *The Commissioners are desired by the Secretary of State to express their appreciation of the way in which you, the medical officer, have carried out your trying and difficult duties in connection with the Suffragist prisoners during the last few weeks. The Secretary of State observes: 'A difficult period has been got through most satisfactorily, owing to the efficiency of the prison service and the carefulness and the good sense shown by the staff.' In conveying this message of commendation the Commissioners desire to express their commendation of the tact, care, humanity, and firmness with which this new and difficult problem has been and is being handled by all concerned.*

The hosepipe incident proved a key turning point in Emily's career in militancy. She wrote afterwards of her realisation, while the prison guards were forcibly breaking down the door to her cell, that 'if the door fell, it would kill me on the spot'. Instead of moving, she had remained in position where she sat – not willing the door to fall on her, but nonetheless revealing a willingness to sacrifice herself if it did. It was the first time Davison showed herself prepared to die for the cause. Her urge to sacrifice anything for her cause was one that would only grow stronger.

She was now engaged in almost constant militancy for the cause. On 4 September 1909 Davison had been arrested with Dora Marsden, a prominent suffragette who had also worked in education and resigned her post – that of headmistress – to work full-time for the WSPU earlier that year. The pair had thrown balls labelled 'bomb' through the window of a meeting room in Old Trafford, Manchester. They received two-month prison sentences in Strangeways, but after undertaking a hunger strike, Davison was released after just two and a half days. Marsden refused to wear prison clothing and was stripped naked, struggling against any efforts made to dress her. The prison wardens eventually forced her into a straitjacket, but she managed to wriggle out of this since she was, as the governor later explained, 'a very small woman'. She too was released after undertaking a hunger strike. Marsden later left the WSPU, partly because of the Pankhursts' autocratic ways, and partly because she came to believe it was dominated by too limited a clique of wealthy women.

In total Emily was arrested on five occasions and served four prison terms during 1909. Letters she wrote around this time revealed that she was revelling both in her activities and the notoriety that accompanied them. On 3 November 1909, she wrote to her friend, Mary Leigh, from 164 Oxford Road, Manchester. The warmth of her tone is testimony to the special closeness of their relationship, while Davison's dismissive reference to the hosepipe incident points to the sense of bravado of a seasoned insurgent.

My dear Mary,

Thanks ever so much for your jolly letter. Your words of praise are far too kind, as are true of others. The point is that I had an absolutely unique chance and did not miss it. My star was in the ascendant. How are you all at 4 Clements' Inn? My love to all! What ages since I have seen you all! ... I have certainly seen some life since I last saw you.

How is your sister?

My love to you!

Davison signed off 'Yours in the cause', and at the bottom of the letter, with increasingly revolutionary zeal, she spurred on her friend and comrade with the addition: 'NO SUR-RENDER! Bravo! ... Mrs Leigh!'

While prison stints took their physical and emotional toll, Davison appeared to enjoy the thrill of prison and the cycle of arrests. In one letter to her friend Dr Ethel Williams, a long-standing non-militant campaigner for suffrage from as early as 1889, who also boasted the dual distinction of being Newcastle's first female doctor and the first woman in the region to drive a car, Davison declared: 'All hail Newcastle, how I wish I were in gaol there!'

CHAPTER 6

THE WOMAN IN PARLIAMENT
1910–1911

A nti-suffrage sentiment grew as the suffragettes scaled up their attacks. Their detractors on the political stage, eager to promote any reason why women should not be given the vote, leapt on the increasing militancy. The siege of vandalism and violence was proof, the suffragettes' critics maintained, of women's inherent instability and predisposition towards hysteria, and a key reason why they should not be granted a role in public life. Conservative MP Arnold Ward, a public advocate for the Women's National Anti-Suffrage League, an organisation his mother had founded, declared to Parliament in 1910 that women 'will act in precisely the same manner to obtain any other political object, whether it be the diminution of public-houses, or Free Trade, or Protection'. The suffragettes' ultimate proposition was, he declared, 'to incorporate that hysterical activity permanently in the life of the nation'.

Not only were women excluded from the vote, they also faced opposition to their participation in debate and decision-making around non-parliamentary matters that directly affected them. When the Royal Commission on Divorce was set up in 1909, King Edward VII was against the appointment of any woman because, he claimed, divorce raised matters which 'cannot be discussed openly and in all its aspects with any delicacy or even decency before ladies.' Public life was merely a wider application of the convention, which carried on for decades after women did gain the vote, whereby ladies were expected to retire from the dining room after dinner to allow the men present to engage in serious and weighty conversations.

The King was far from the only proponent of such preju-dices. Society in the first and second decade of the twentieth century harboured a significant proportion of men who thought women constitutionally and intellectually unfit for public life, and therefore unworthy of a ballot. Among the most vocal and forthright of opponents of female suf-frage was Sir Almroth Wright, a scientist who became a pioneer in the study of antibiotics and discovered that their overuse would create resistant strains of disease. Although distinguished in his field, he was a stanch reactionary when it came to women's right to vote. In a 3,850-word letter to *The Times*, headlined 'Letter on Militant Hysteria', he asserted that women were subject to monthly bouts of unreason and claimed: 'There is mixed up with the women's movement much mental disorder.'

He went on to diagnose what he saw as the different kinds of suffragette, among whom, he said, were 'women who have all their life-long been strangers to joy, women in whom instincts long suppressed have in the end broken into flame. These are the sexually embittered women in whom everything has turned into gall and bitterness of heart, and hatred of men'. He then identified 'the woman who is poisoned by her misplaced self-esteem; and who flies out at every man who does not pay homage to her intellect.' His conclusion was: 'The evils of woman suffrage [sic] lie, *first*, in the fact that to give the vote to women is to give it to voters who as a class are quite incompetent to adjudicate upon political issues'. He added that enfranchising women 'may seriously embroil man and woman.' As it happens, *The Times* had long agreed with the views of Sir Almroth Wright and his allies, writing leaders such as one in 1906 which asserted 'the unfitness of women to enter public life'.

Wright even went so far as to publish a book setting out what he obviously thought were the clinching arguments against women's rights. Called 'The Unexpurgated Case Against Women's Suffrage', it was one of many similar publications; another popular book in the genre was 'The Anti-Suffrage Handbook of Facts, Statistics and Quotations For The Use of Speakers'. This was produced in 1912 by the National League for Opposing Woman Suffrage, itself one of the signs that opposition to female enfranchisement, from 1906 onwards, become much better organised.

Many women joined the ranks of the male anti-suffrage

campaigners too, and in July 1908 the Women's National Anti-Suffrage League was founded. Prominent among its leadership was Caroline Stephen, Virginia Woolf's aunt. The organisation later merged in 1910 with the men's group. Among other prominent women against the vote were Katharine Stewart-Murray, Marchioness of Tullibardine, who later became an MP and is better known today by her final title the Duchess of Atholl; Mrs Humphry Ward, a popular novelist of the time; Gertrude Bell, a traveller and writer; and Beatrice Webb, the socialist writer (though she later changed her views).

As the new decade dawned, further political setbacks lay in wait for the suffragettes. Chancellor Lloyd George, who had been an early supporter of women's suffrage, had made a volte-face on the subject. He was enraged by the heckling of suffragette campaigners who would verbally attack him as a minister of the government for ignoring their cause. He had ordered, when touring the country giving speeches to try to whip up support for his radical Budget (which the Lords were threatening to block), that the audiences should include no women. From a party political perspective, Lloyd George also came to believe unshakeably that the extension of votes to women in national elections would favour the Conservatives over his own Liberal Party.

Infuriated by the Chancellor's change of heart, the suffragettes began to target him personally. Davison took to writing him letters. One such missive read: 'My conviction is that you will never get really good, effective measures for housing, for temperance and social reform, until you get millions of women to cooperate in such legislation. Why don't you counsel women when you bring forward reforming legislation?'

Davison was infuriated by the lack of progress the WSPU was making in the political arena. Prime Minister Asquith had successfully avoided addressing women's suffrage at all and excused the oversight by citing the House of Lords reforms to which he devoted his attention. She resolved, therefore, to penetrate the House of Commons and to ask Asquith directly why, when he was denouncing the action of the Lords, he would not make the House of Commons more representative by giving the vote to women taxpayers. She determined to elicit an answer as to why, before attempting to reform the House of Lords, he had not set his own House in order.

She resolved to smuggle herself into a private area in the Houses of Parliament and confront him. Just after lunch one April afternoon, she followed two ladies in Old Palace Yard. When she arrived at the Great Central Hall, she saw to her joy doors to a passage leading out of the hall marked 'Private'. The policeman on duty was engaged in conversation, so Emily tried one of the doors. It opened and she crept into the private passageway. The police report later located the passageway as the 'vestibule adjoining Strangers Dining Room, Smoking Room Corridor, House of Commons which is approached by South East door lower waiting hall'.

Davison later wrote:

In the wall I saw a little glass window with a knob, and when I opened it I looked into a dark place which was very hot, and found it was the heating apparatus of the Houses. I got in and closed the window. There was a series of ladders going up higher and higher into the tower. I climbed up the first with difficulty, as the place was narrow, and reached the first platform.

When she was high enough up the tower, she decided to hide there on a platform within. She reported:

Then came a period of hideous, awful waiting. The time wore away so slowly, for I had nothing to do but think and read my guide to the Houses of Parliament. I was terribly afraid of being discovered, especially as I had a cold which I could not altogether check with lozenges. It was almost overpoweringly hot. The only provisions I had were two bananas and some chocolate. The latter and the lozenges, together with the heat, gradually made me thirsty. I was tired and yet in too uncomfortable a position to sleep. I was also afraid of tumbling over into the well below. Luckily, [at] about 7 o'clock some of the pipes were turned off, and I even began to feel cold, so that I put on my jacket again and huddled up. The place was indescribably filthy. Years of dirt and dust lay on everything. My face, clothes and head were begrimed. Every now and again with great care I stood up to allay the aching of my bones. Big Ben kept me informed of the slow progress of time, and occasionally I heard the footsteps of some distant watchman.

At last, about 4 o'clock, morning light began to dawn, and I was truly thankful. Hour by hour passed on, till about 7 o'clock the hot pipes were turned on again. As the day wore on and the heat increased, my sufferings from thirst became so intense that I felt that even if I risked being seized I must descend and look for water. It was the first time that I had left my perch.

At 1.45 I descended. Arrived at the bottom, I opened the glass window cautiously and looked out. No one was about. To my joy I saw just below the window a tap with a little tin dish below it, and 'Cold' printed above it. I climbed out, and, as all was silent, eagerly drank some water. It was indescribably comforting. I rubbed some over my begrimed face and hands. I dare not stay, so swallowing as much as I could of the blessed water, I crept back into the hiding-place and up the shaft. After that I felt capable of waiting on for days, if necessary. I dozed occasionally and listened for the Abbey afternoon service bells. Later on, however, I had to go down again for another drink. Four, five, and six o'clock struck, and once more I felt the need of water. I descended, alas for the last time. I drank the cool, blessed water eagerly. Then I noticed that as the dish was narrow and flat a good deal of water was spilt on the floor, and fervently hoped no one would pass that way.

I had just returned to my niche when I heard steps

and saw light, for the evening was closing in. I drew back as far as I could, but, of course, the water attracted the watchman's eyes. He opened the door and looked in, and there he saw me. What I must have appeared to be I cannot say – a terrible object no doubt. The poor constable was terror-stricken, so that he nearly dropped his lantern. He trembled violently, and called out, 'What is it?' He banged the window to, and then he seized his whistle and blew it shrilly. Still trembling, he opened the door again and yelled: 'Come out!' When I descended, he gripped me hard and drew me out of the passage, and there at least appeared another constable, very much astonished.

After I had washed I was taken quietly to Cannon Row by the station passage, and had a meal which was brought to me by the matron, while they sent in every direction to find a friend who would bail me out, and at last, about 9.30, a constable came in and told me that I was free to go. I could hardly believe it, but found that the authorities had decided not to prosecute me. It appears that I could not have been tried in a police court, but would have to appear before the House of Commons itself; this is probably the reason I was not prosecuted. I went back to my lodgings to recover cleanliness and ordinary comfort. Such was my visit to the House of Commons!

The man who found her was PC Horndike. The official police report, dated 4 April, recorded:

He found a woman standing on a ladder in the shaft just above the temporary staging fitted up from workmen. He said 'What are you doing here?' She said: 'I am a Suffragette and my ambition is to get into the House to ask a question'. PC asked else [*sic*] if anyone else was in the shaft. She said: 'No, I am entirely on my own'. I asked her why she went into the shaft. She said: 'I want to ask a question in the House of Commons tomorrow' … Her face and hands were black and her clothing very dirty. She asked to have a wash, which she had. She then gave the name of Emily Davison, 4 Clement's Inn, Strand, teacher.

Davison, however, had left her mark on Parliament. The police report documenting the incident noted:

The following was found written in pencil on a window pane '3rd April 1910. Patience. 36 hours here. Will they ever go. I am so thirsty. Nearly 36 hours have gone and I found water Thank God. E W Davison April 10. Rebellion against Tyrants is obedience to God.'

In addition to her scrawling on parliamentary property, Davison began writing articles and reviews for the WSPU newspaper, *Votes for Women*. Among her contributions during this year was an article about a megaphone parade in which she had participated and a review of the Japanese-British Exhibition in London. She also wrote short biographies of social reformers, Florence Nightingale and Elizabeth Fry, the religious writer Hannah More and a series of female abolitionists. As a student of literature she enjoyed putting her creative writing skills to use. Of course she was not, as a woman, permitted to professions in which she might have exercised her intelligence in other ways. She remained a regular contributor to the suffragette press until December 1911. Her dedication to the cause was noticed and it was this that won her paid employment with the WSPU.

That summer, a temporary truce was agreed between the suffragettes and the government. The reason for this particular suspension of hostilities is unclear, but, as historian Sir Brian Harrison notes, while it did not last, the pause in the militant programme meant that its resumption proved newsworthy. The battle for media coverage was one of the most important in the suffragettes' war, but it was not the only driving force behind the militancy. Davison herself explained the strategy in a letter to the editor of the *Yorkshire Observer* in November 1911: 'You seem to think that the mere raison d'etre of militancy is advertisement. That, of course, follows, but it is not, and never has been, the chief reason for militancy. Militancy means in plain language determination to win at all costs.'[18]

Politicians were concerned that the suffragettes' thirst for column inches in newspapers was fuelling the escalation and theatrics of their militant acts. Home Secretary Reginald McKenna was aggrieved by the press attention they won, and later in 1914, made public his belief that if the reports of their actions had been stifled, the incidents themselves would have immediately ceased. The press did not, however, take kindly to the politician's interference in their business. *The Globe*, then London's oldest evening newspaper, lambasted his 'effrontery' in complaining of press reports, while *The Times* wrote: 'The function of newspapers is, after all, to supply news and tell the public what is going on. Regard for ulterior consequences may be carried too far.'

By June the suffragettes were growing weary and frustrated at Asquith's delaying tactics. On 18 June, the various organisations of the countrywide women's suffrage movement joined forces to demonstrate against the government and demand that a bill be passed swiftly. Asquith responded in the House of Commons five days later, giving little hope for optimism among the suffragettes. Davison was among hundreds of women incensed by his obstruction of their cause. That evening she hurled chunks of chalk wrapped with messages of intent at the Crown Office, breaking two panes of glass. She was arrested and again offered an alternative to a prison sentence: a £5 fine. She resolutely refused the get-out option and prepared to enter prison again, but mysteriously the money was paid without her knowledge or permission and she walked away free. It is possible a politician or an 'anti' paid the fine in a bid to starve her of publicity.[xii]

It was likely around the time of the truce that Davison

---

xii   It was widely believed that in 1905 Winston Churchill, then a backbench MP, had attempted to pay fines levied on Christabel Pankhurst and Annie Kenney to secure their freedom and avoid them galvanising support from jail cells. If it is true he attempted the feat, he was unsuccessful.

went up to Longhorsley to spend some time at her mother's home. There was a deep bond between the two, and Davison took much comfort from her mother's company. Her respite did not last long, however, for the suffragettes were to suffer their most crushing political setback yet. In November 1910, Asquith announced his plan to shelve the Women's Suffrage Bill for good. Pankhurst organised a demonstration at the House of Commons on 18 November. Davison's contemporary biographer described 'sickening scenes' at the protest, remarking on the 'coarse roughness of the police and of the hooligan element, encouraged by the police; the orgie of brutality which has caused the name of Black Friday to be given to that day'.

One suffragette named Henria Helen L. Williams, a campaigner living in Essex, suffered barbaric treatment at the hands of a policeman, reporting afterwards:

> One policeman, after knocking me about for a considerable time, finally took hold of me with his great strong hand like iron just over my heart. He hurt me so much that at first I had not the voice power to tell him what he was doing. But I knew that unless I made a strong effort to do so he would kill me. So collecting all the power of my being, I commanded him to take his hand off my heart … He was the third or fourth who had knocked me about.

Henria died some months later. Cecelia Wolseley-Haig, a scion of the Haig whisky family, also died in 1911 from injuries sustained on Black Friday. In light of their deaths, and that of Emmeline Pankhurst's sister, Mary Clark, following force-feeding, it is wrong to characterise Davison as the sole martyr of the movement.[19] She remains the best-known, however, and was the only one of the four to be honoured with a public funeral.

Charles Mansell Moullin, who was a male sympathiser and married to Davison's friend Edith, was present at the scene on Black Friday. In a letter to *The Times* published the next day, he said:

> *I was a witness at yesterday's peaceful rally outside the Houses of Parliament when I saw the women marchers treated with the greatest brutality; they were pushed about in all directions and thrown down by the police; their arms were twisted until they were almost broken, their thumbs were forcibly bent back and they were tortured in other unnameless ways that made one feel sick inside. These things were done by the police and since their behaviour is an entirely new departure, it would be interesting to know if they had been instructed to act with such brutality by some higher authority.*[20]

Black Friday marked a turning point in the WSPU's campaign strategy. From that point onwards, the leaders of the movement decided their members should no longer undertake deputations and risk violent retaliation from the police. Instead they would resort to stone-throwing and vandalism to make their point.

Davison had escaped arrest in this instance, but the next

day returned to the House of Commons and smashed more windows. She was livid at the treatment of her comrades the day before and devastated by Asquith's response to the promised Conciliation Bill. This time she was arrested, tried eleven days later, and once again offered a fine or prison sentence. She chose prison and was sent to Holloway. There she was denied exercise, communication with her peers, and crushingly, access to the prison chapel. She went on hunger strike and two days later was forcibly fed in the punishment cells. Six days later she was released.

By spring 1911 Davison purported to be optimistic about the WSPU's eventual triumph. In March she wrote to the editor of the *Sunday Times*:

> *It is not physical force nowadays which rules the world, and that is why the women will win. They will win it probably through intense suffering to themselves, some of which they have already gone through in taking up this terrible fight against convention and prejudice, which has led them to face ridicule, abuse, personal ill-treatment, indecency, deadly insult, which has led them to face exposure and discomfort, to face the hunger-strike, and that 'torture of tortures,' which is not practiced in Russia, forcible feeding, besides other sacrifices which will never be known, not to speak of the loss of friends, position, and livelihood. Women have all along faced the fact that in order to win the final victory some of their number may probably have to pay the last and extreme penalty, because physical force is still so strong. They have faced it already, and*

will face it again, and therein lies their power. They have the moral courage to face it! Christianity itself is an evidence that physical force does not rule the world. This nation has a conscience and cannot afford to have its fair name forever sullied in the eyes of the civilised world.[21]

Soon after writing this letter, Davison was plotting again to break into Parliament. This time, it was mischievously to disrupt the April 1911 census, the once-a-decade counting of every Briton, which many suffragettes, and a few men, boycotted in protest at the lack of the vote for women. So, on the evening of the count, she hid in the cupboard in the crypt of the Palace of Westminster, in a cupboard next to the Chapel of St Mary Undercroft. She spent the night there so she could record the Palace of Westminster on her form as her temporary residence. She snuck into the crypt under Westminster Hall, narrowly escaping the notice of an MP showing visitors around, and shut the door behind her. It locked. It was not until a cleaner discovered her that she was able to get out. The police arrived and took Davison once again to Cannon Row station. She was detained for just a few hours, however, before being dismissed. In the event she was, perhaps unknown to herself, recorded twice in the census, in the second instance being registered as a lodger in a house near St Pancras at 31 Coram Street.

Her stunt tied in with the efforts of hundreds of suffragettes to protest their lack of political rights by refusing to fill in the census forms. Davison wrote on her own census form: 'As I am a woman and women do not count in the State, I refuse to be counted.' Then followed her motto: 'Rebellion against tyrants is obedience to god.' In June, she was again arrested for being within the confines of the House of Commons, and, in the record of the subsequent court appearance, 'supposed for the purpose of committing a breach of the peace.' She told the magistrate that the 'breach of the peace' consisted in an intention to address the House and there being no evidence to show that she intended to attack anybody, she was discharged, but refused, however, to give an undertaking not to return.

Subverting the census was an easy task and therefore a tactic favoured by the 'non-heroic many', as historian Maureen Howes has pointed out, adding that some male suffragists such as Laurence Housman also joined in.[22]

Later that year Davison was said to have been arrested with suffragette Charlotte Marsh for breaking windows on Regent Street in London's West End.[23] As well as partaking in vandalism in the area, she also visited it to attend the theatre during the autumn of 1911. In *Votes for Women* she wrote a review of *The Perplexed Husband* by Alfred Sutro, a popular production that was on at Wyndham's Theatre.

Her review offers an insight not only into her own views but what she saw as the prevailing orthodoxies of the day regarding the women's suffrage movement. She wrote:

There is no doubt whatever that Votes for Women is the burning question of the day, beside which all others pale in interest. The very fact that Mr. Sutro, one of our most popular playwrights, has chosen to weave his modern comedy of manners round the Woman question is proof positive, if any were needed, of the primary importance of the question. Even the most Anti of dramatists cannot get away from the all-absorbing topic...

The underlying motif of 'The Perplexed Husband' is the idea that Woman Suffrage means the destruction of household peace and happiness. Suffragists, of course, know quite well that this is radically wrong. The result of the enfranchisement of women will be an elevation of the home-life of the country, for there will be fewer loveless marriages, when women, being established in a sound, economic position, will no longer make a trade of one of the highest of human ideals...

The Suffragist [character], Dulcie Elstead, is completely feminist and anti-man. This betrays the most serious lack of comprehension of the real meaning of the movement, which all true supporters know to be an evolutionary one, for the advancement not of women alone, but of the whole race. John Stuart Mill showed that no race could rise above its women. If the nation is to progress, the women must rise. Thus when Dulcie Elstead proclaims herself to be 'feminist, rebel and Suffragist', she is belying the whole movement.[24]

She got into her stride during the autumn of 1911; hitting back against the social constructs she felt had been imposed upon women. In September she wrote to the editor of the *Morning Post* to complain about 'the men who trained up women in the idea that they were either to be over-dressed, unintellectual dolls, or miserably underpaid and ill-treated drudges. Women were either on a pedestal or in the mire. But this artificial absurdity is rapidly passing away'.[25]

Meanwhile in a letter to the *Yorkshire Weekly Post* she said:

For centuries and centuries the faculty of initiative has been absolutely taboo to 'women'. Their education (if it might be so termed), surroundings and influences were impossible soil for the rearing of originality. They were trained up in one groove only, one inexorable routine, that of preparing to be housewives for their husbands, and the only possible departure from that groove was to train to be the spouse of the Church, a not very dissimilar vocation.

In this period of prolific writing output, Davison returned several times to the subject of female workers' rights. In one letter to the press about female Bermondsey strikers,[xiii] she offered an insight into the satisfaction she derived from undertaking militant actions as a free woman even though they led to ordeals in prison. She wrote: 'What the girls enjoyed and what the Suffragettes have enjoyed in undergoing their

---

xiii   Landmark strikes took place in Bermondsey in 1911 as 15,000 women working across twenty-three factories in the food-processing industry resorted to industrial action to win concessions on pay and conditions.

most horrible experiences has been that joy in at last asserting their individuality as free-born Britons.'

In another letter she addressed the travails of the so-called pit brow women, the female surface labourers at British collieries. Since 1842 women had been prevented from working deep in coal mines, but in 1911 the government sought to extend this ban to the girls and women who worked above ground. The suffragettes showed solidarity with the women who faced the prospect of losing their livelihood. Davison wrote: 'The action of the Miners' Federation with regard to women's labour at the pit brow only affords further proof, if any were required, of the necessity of women having direct representation. These men, on the specious plea of sentimentalism, assume their right to interfere in women's labour.'[26]

In another letter she surmised that the British character was 'extremely cautious and slow to change', blaming this for the sluggish progress of the women's enfranchisement movement since its inception in the 1870s. Detailing her solution to shock the system out of its stasis, she said:

In order to make John Bull[xiv] move it has been proved in the past that he must be given an electric shock. He got it in the uprising of his womenfolk. That women should stand up and demand justice was, to the slow-going old gentleman, absolutely unthinkable. He opened his eyes; he wondered if he were standing on his head or his heels. But the shock had succeeded in its object;

---

xiv   The personification of the United Kingdom in general, and England in particular.

it had roused him. Now the result of the shock was this: John
Bull was first pained and surprised; he then was led to examine
the matter; and the last stage is conversion. He is hovering be-
tween the last two stages now, but he has at any rate reached the
stage of interest. That is well shown in the Press...

With the dawn of liberty ahead of them they [women] are
struggling upwards, but it is a bitter fight. One by one they are
breaking the fetters and gradually gaining power. The day is
not far distant when they will stand free, side by side by men,
untrammeled, erect, with the proud bearing of equals; diverse,
yet equal.[27]

In December Davison put down her pen to develop an exciting new tactic: setting pillar boxes alight. She would soak
a cloth in paraffin in advance, then light it on approach to a
pillar box and roughly shove it through the slit. In one such
incident in London, she set a letterbox alight before calmly
walking into a nearby café and taking lunch, while the postbox she left behind her billowed black smoke. Soon copycat
acts occurred up and down the country. When charged at
Bow Street, she confessed to other attacks and said: 'I did
this entirely on my own responsibility'. She was released on
bail, amused to learn the authorities thought her security
worth £1,000 (the amount of the fixed bail). Davison left
London to spend Christmas at Longhorsley.

At the time Sylvia Pankhurst denied that the letterbox firings
were performed in accordance with the WSPU's programme
of sabotage and vandalism. Such a public proclamation in

itself indicates the leadership's displeasure at Davison breaking rank. Yet although she was acting by her own initiative, her
act was to inspire a series of similar incendiarism.

Sylvia Pankhurst wrote in her 1931 book, *The Suffrage
Movement*:

> Militancy was now assuming a new and serious aspect. In
> December 1911 and March 1912, Emily Wilding Davison
> and Nurse Pitfield had committed spectacular arson on
> their own initiative, both doing their deeds openly and
> suffering arrest and punishment ... When the policy was
> fully under way, certain officials of the Union were given,
> as their main work, the task of advising incendiaries, and
> arranging for the supply of such inflammable material,
> housebreaking tools, and other matters as they might re-
> quire. A certain exceedingly feminine-looking young lady
> was strolling about London, meeting militants in all sorts of
> public and unexpected places, to arrange for perilous expe-
> ditions. Women, most of them very young, toiled through
> the night across unfamiliar country, carrying heavy cases
> of petrol and paraffin. Sometimes they failed, sometimes
> succeeded in setting fire to an untenanted building – all the
> better if it were the residence of a notability – or a church,
> or other place of historic interest. Occasionally they were
> caught and convicted; usually they escaped.

One of the premier reasons for the suffragettes to upgrade their
militancy was to elicit greater publicity. Historian Sir Brian

Harrison concluded: 'To the militant rank and file, escalated militancy seems a natural response to injustice and oppression; for the leaders, by contrast, its major merit is publicity.' The group's violent tactics were shocking to the establishment. Never before in British history had a dissident movement – pioneered by women and for women – arisen. It was, for many, an unsettling development. Some labelled the suffragettes the biggest threat to the survival of the British Empire. As Harrison notes, by March 1907 plain-clothes policemen had been dispatched to shadow WSPU leaders, while by September 1909, the Metropolitan Police expanded their ranks in order to provide heightened security for government ministers, whom they believed to be at high risk of attack by suffragettes.

It is now known that long-lens photography was pioneered specifically as a surveillance instrument against the suffragettes. Declassified Home Office files reveal that the police spied on suffragettes using what was, at the time, cutting-edge technology: a Ross Telecentric camera with an eleven-inch lens. A professional photographer named Mr Barrett was commissioned to take the pictures 'concealed in a prison van' in the exercise yard in Holloway Prison so that militants could be identified at any future demonstrations or committing acts of violence.

Lilian Lenton was one of many women who were repeatedly arrested as a result of being recognised by policemen from their surveillance photographs. Documents in the files prove that the women's suffrage movement was the first 'terrorist' organisation subjected to secret surveillance photography in the United Kingdom, if not the world.

Whether the most extreme suffragettes were dangerous terrorists or brave pioneers remains a live debate. While many people today accept that they were fighting for a just cause – equal rights for men and women – the bombing campaign they undertook involved a strong degree of risk to human life. Explosive devices were planted at Westminster Abbey, St Paul's Cathedral and the Royal Observatory in Edinburgh, where a great deal of damage was caused.

However, as Mary Leigh recalled decades later: 'Mrs Pankhurst gave us strict orders … there was not a cat or a canary to be killed: no life.' Pankhurst's biographer Professor June Purvis has argued that those who claim the suffragettes were terrorists are 'misguided and sensationalist', adding: 'They are simply seeking to condemn these radical women who were campaigning for their democratic right to the parliamentary vote.'

Nonetheless, while their methods bear little resemblance to those used by terrorists in modern times, many suffragettes themselves applied the label of terrorism to their tactics. Alongside planting bombs, the most extreme of these tactics included setting fire to postboxes, sports pavilions, Lloyd George's empty country cottage in Walton Heath in Surrey and even cutting the telegraph line from London to Glasgow. Laura Wilson, a suffragette weaver from Halifax, told a reporter at the time: 'I went to jail a rebel, but I have come out a regular terror.'

Davison was charged with committing arson on 14 December 1911 and openly confessed it. She told the police:

Certainly, the matchbox was not wrapped up in the linen and paper. That was a separate package. I used one of the matches, then threw the box in. I set the linen packet alight. I threw first the packet in, then the matchbox. A boy saw me do it. You quite understand there was a witness to the Mansion House case. A man saw it. He stopped for a minute.

She set out her rationale for the arson campaign in an essay, titled 'Incendiarism' in late 1911.[xv] She described Asquith's recently declared intention to introduce a Manhood Suffrage Bill, which would extend the male franchise while still neglecting to empower women, as 'unpardonable' and 'the last straw'. The suffragettes' response to the news had been to convene a protest in Parliament Square. There, both Lady Constance Lytton and Mary Leigh were arrested. The aristocrat was treated 'most indulgently' and sentenced to a fortnight in prison, Davison noted, while Leigh, whose only crime had been to deface property, was handed a two-month sentence. 'This made my blood boil. The injustice and snobbery was so great,' Davison wrote.

She went on:

However I thought that something would be done to avenge it. Nothing was done, and I resolved to take it upon myself to make a protest. This couldn't be done at once, as

---

xv   Appendix 3.

I was engaged in secretarial work. But soon I resolved to stake all. On December 1st, 1911 I gave notice to leave and began laying my plans. I resolved that this time damage should be done that could not be repaired. The next step to window breaking was incendiarism. On December 8th, when I was free, at lunch time I walked down the Strand to Fleet Street. When I arrived at the Fleet Street P.O. which faces Fetter Lane I calmly stopped at the big open mouthed receptacle for London letters, I took out of my pocket a packet of the same size as an ordinary letter. It was of grease-proof paper tied with cotton. Inside was some linen well soaked in kerosene. One corner of the paper was torn so as to let out the kerosene rag ready. To this I calmly applied a match, which I had struck on a box of matches, and held it for a second. A small boy was passing by and stopped short on seeing what I was doing. I let the packet, now well alight, go down the receptacle, and threw the matches afterwards. I then quietly walked on down Fleet Street and turned into the first Lyons I came to get lunch. My heart was beating rapidly.[28]

She listened as police whistles blew and was satisfied after returning to the street of the incident to see telegraph boys examining the aperture into which she had thrown the packet and matches. After researching the penalty due to post office or postbox arson – imprisonment of up to a year – she wrote two letters to the press outing herself as the culprit and declaring that she planned to give herself up to the police on Monday morning. She posted the letters in a pillar box outside St Paul's and then attended a service there.

She followed through with her plan, but upon confessing to a constable, said she was told by the policeman that 'I cannot arrest you ... I should not think of giving you such an advertisement for your cause'. She went on: 'Seeing that public authorities did not mean to prosecute, I walked away. Later on I phoned up the Press and explained what had happened. The thought now in my mind was that I must carry out the protest so strongly that it could not be ignored. I laid my plans accordingly.'

Davison then went on to 'fire two pillar boxes in the City'. She called up the London News Office and told them her next plan was to arson a post office. She asked the journalists whether they thought the General Post Office or Parliament Street a more effective target.

> They very agitatedly said they could not possibly give advice. Feeling amused and seeing the truth of this, for they would otherwise have been accessories to my act, I answered, 'Of course not I ought to have thought of that! Well! I shall do my deed to be caught at one or the other between 1 and 2 o'clock,' then rang off. I then went and had a good lunch at Slater's near Knightsbridge and dawdled the time between 12 and 1 o'clock. At 1 o'clock I sallied forth. It was a glorious day and I walked to Hyde Park Corner. I looked at the clock. Time seemed to be going on, so I took a bus to Trafalgar Square. There I got down

and took another bus down Whitehall. My reason for doing this was that if I walked down I might be spotted by detectives who would probably be on the look out for me and who might prevent me doing any thing at all. As I had said to the Press, I wished to be caught 'in the act.' My bus stopped at Bridge Street. I got down. As I turned into Parliament Street, I first came across Superintendent Wells, who looked at me curiously. I then came right facing Inspector Powell and Constable City 185, both in private clothes. They looked at me, but I was glad they were coming towards me, as they could not turn too ostentatiously. I however went on past them up to the Post Office. I stood there, and quickly took out of my pocket one of my kerosene packets, struck a match and lit it deliberately and put it in. That did not burn well, and I was not yet arrested, so I took out another and even more ostentatiously set it alight and tried to put it into the letter box. By this time Powell had seen what I was up to. He reached forward literally grabbed the thing out of my hand, blew it out, seized me violently and said, 'I knew you would do this, Miss Davison.' Cn 185 City seized me on the other side and they rushed me into Cannon Row Police Station. As we went I called out, 'I am arrested, friends.'[29]

The letterbox arsons were a significant landmark in Davison's insurgency. They also indicate her decision to go rogue and deviate from strict WSPU guidelines. During her subsequent prison time, her willingness to make the sacrifice of her life also became clear for the second time following the hosepipe incident in 1909. Davison expressed an increasing sense of urgency about making progress in the cause. Unable to bear the suffering of so many of her comrades and ground down by the cycle of militancy, arrests and hunger strikes, her regard for her own safety diminished as her desire to see her cause triumph increased. From this time onwards, she demonstrated more manifestly the psychology of the martyr.

CHAPTER 7

THE TORTURE OF FORCE-FEEDING 1911–1912

D avison spent Christmas and New Year of 1911 with her mother in Longhorsley. By all accounts this was an idyllic period for the pair, during which suffrage, tactics and militancy were subjects left untouched. Instead, they enjoyed each other's company and relaxed. One evening, Davison and her mother lolled by the roaring fire in the cottage and passed the time singing hymns; 'Thy Way, Not Mine, O Lord' and 'Fight The Good Fight With All Thy Might' were their songs of choice. Later that year, in a moment when she was feeling particularly low, Davison wrote to her mother recalling the happiness of that day.

On 7 January 1912, she returned to London to fight her arson court case, which commenced two days later. Despite the reprieve that Davison had allowed herself during the Christmas holiday, she was about to enter a heavy period of militancy, which would last until her death eighteen months later. Intense as her personal campaign was, she also became increasingly reflective during this time, writing a number of thoughtful and personal essays. First she had to stand trial for her postbox arson attempts, however. She had already taken responsibility for the actions and pleaded guilty. She arrived at the courthouse with her close friends, the couple Eleanor and George Penn Gaskell. To their delight and amusement, the court was besieged with sympathisers who had turned out to support Davison, by now a famous face of the suffrage movement.

The authorities were less pleased to see such a crowd, and, purportedly in a bid to prevent disruption to the case, declared all women banned from the courtroom. Davison was outraged, not least because she had counted on the moral support of her companion, Eleanor Penn Gaskell, from the benches of the court. Her husband valiantly attempted to have the order overturned, but the court authorities were adamant. Penn Gaskell was forced to wait outside the courtroom and listen ignominiously at the door. After the opening procedures had commenced, however, she was puzzled to hear her own name called from within the court. The doors were hauled open and she found herself led up to the witness box, called to testify on behalf of the defence. Bemused, she caught Davison's eye and the stunt was understood. Coolly, the suffragette on trial began to put questions to her friend, but her queries were so banal that the judge, infuriated, terminated the examination of the witness. Davison had achieved her aim, however: Eleanor Penn Gaskell had been admitted into the courtroom and there she remained until the end of the hearing.

Inspector Francis Powell, a policeman from New Scotland Yard, was among the witnesses for the prosecution. He testified against Davison:

On December 14, I was in Parliament Street from 1.20 p.m. near the post office. I saw the prisoner walk from the pavement up to the letterbox at the post office, which stands slightly back from the pavement ... When she got close to the letterbox her head was stooped and she appeared to be striking matches. I rushed up behind her and looked over her shoulder. She was holding a small packet in the left hand, one of the top corners of which was slightly alight. She held it in that position for a minute as if to give it an opportunity of becoming more alight. It touched the aperture of the letterbox. I seized the packet with my left hand and in doing so extinguished the flame. I took her into custody to New Scotland Yard. When there, she sat in a room. As I was leaving the room she called me back and said, 'Do you know I set fire to two in the City this morning, a pillar-box in the middle of Leadenhall Street – it burned ... as what I put in was well alight and it was the most effective; the other was facing the Mansion House and Mappin and Webb's. I confess that I set fire to a post office, 43, Fleet Street, on Friday last and on the Monday following I went up to a policeman to be arrested.'

EMILY WILDING DAVISON

I asked her if she had seen the policeman since and she said, 'No, but I know his number, it is 185.' She immediately corrected herself and said, 'Why, he is sitting there.' As a matter of fact he was in the room in plain clothes. At Scotland Yard I said that 'I knew you would do something to a post office from your past history. At the time I was not expecting to see you. I know nothing against your character beyond certain matters connected with the movement to which you belong: I believe it to be a good one. You had no object of personal spite in this matter. I do not know whether you had anything to gain in this matter.'

It is striking that a senior police officer, such as Inspector Powell, who would be one of the suffragettes' natural enemies, should testify as to Davison's good character beyond the movement.

The suffragette herself then spoke to the court:

My motive in doing this was to protest against the vindictive sentence and treatment that my comrade, Mary Leigh, when she was last charged at this Court received, compared with the treatment awarded to Lady Constance Lytton, who has done far more damage. Secondly, I wished to call upon the Government to put Women [sic] Suffrage into the King's Speech on 14 February, 1912. As the protest was meant to be serious, I adopted a serious course. In the agitation for reform in the past, the next step after window breaking was incendiaries in order to draw the attention of the private citizen to the fact that the question of reform is their concern as well as that of women.

Three points I wish to make about my act. First, I might have done with perfect ease a great deal more damage than I did. I contented myself with doing just the amount that would make my protest decisive. Secondly, I walked on the Thursday, December 14, into the Aldgate district, but would not do any damage there, because the people were of the poorer class. Thirdly, the reason I offered to give myself up on Monday, December 11, was that I thought Post Office officials might have been suspected of the deed, as there was trouble in the Post Office just then. Finally, women are now so moved upon this question that they feel that anything necessary to be done must be done, regardless of the consequences, but the consequences do not really lie at their door, but at the door of those who have refused to deal with the question as a matter of justice.

…There was no malice in what I did. It was a purely political act and was done from no motive whatever but to draw the attention of the public to the iniquitous state of affairs now existing; and it has long ago been recognised in England that men who do any act of violence from a political motive must be differently treated from those who do it with a purely personal motive: that is the distinction between the political prisoner and the ordinary criminal.

Technically, of course, I suppose I must be judged to be

guilty, but morally I am not guilty; morally it is you before whom I stand who are guilty; you, the private citizens of this country and the Government that you choose to represent, you, who keep women out of their just rights as citizens, and in so doing absolutely prevent your country having the right to be called a democratic country; that is, a country where the rights of the people hold good; and so long as you exclude women from these rights, upon you lies the blame of any act that they may have to commit in order to procure those rights.

When she gave her evidence, Eleanor Penn Gaskell said:

I know the prisoner very well. The motive with which this act was done was decidedly a political motive. I know that all these deeds are simply done to call the attention of the public to the great cause for which we stand. I know the prisoner to be a woman of the very highest character and honour, and that she would not do any deeds of this kind with a personal object.

By this time Emily had six convictions against her, for assault on the police, obstruction of the police, and doing wilful damage, all in connection with the women's suffrage movement. Inspector Powell had already noted, fairly, that: 'She is highly respectable beyond this movement.' He now added: 'She has given the police a great deal of trouble.' Davison was sentenced to six months' imprisonment – her longest prison term yet. Daunted by such an arduously lengthy sentence, she appealed without avail.

In February Davison re-entered Holloway. In the early days of her sentence she wrote an essay, 'The Real Christianity', in which she bristled against the association of motherhood with 'the Hebraic idea of Purification and the necessity to remove a stigma, a defilement'.

Despite her religiosity, she did not demur from criticising the founding narratives of Christianity when she felt they had been weaponised to suppress women. In the essay, among her most cogently argued pieces, she asked of the festival of Candlemas: 'Why should it be called "the Purification of St. Mary the Virgin"? Could the Saint be defiled by a Holy Thing?'[30] The piece went on:

> Even as the Church obscures and disfigures some of her [Mary's] most beautiful truths, so the world at large has travestied and deformed one of the natural blessings of the world, one of the phenomena whereby all things are made new. Thus it is that the office of Motherhood is made both the glory and the humiliation of women. Men will prate about the beauty and dignity of Motherhood in the same breath with which they will hold up this important function as a reason for continuing the subjection of women. When a woman adopts as her natural calling the office of motherhood, she is not treated with reverence as the Life-Bearer, the Vivifier, but as either the toy or the drudge of her mate...

The nation is shortsighted, is committed to a suicidal policy so long as the custodians of life are refused voice in its councils. What wonder that the rate of infantile mortality is rapidly increasing! ... Motherhood is still associated with the Hebraic idea of Purification and the necessity to remove a stigma, a defilement. And as motherhood is the common lot of women, the status of women is still proportionately contemptible.

None of Davison's written work records her views about having – or not having – children herself. By the time of this essay she was approaching the age of forty and would not have expected to be able to have children.

During this stint in prison Davison would, wrote her contemporary biographer, 'pass through a time of suffering greater in length and intensity than any she had yet endured'. Again she was subjected to the horror of force-feeding. This time, however, the brutal, injurious practice was not implemented in response to Davison undertaking hunger strike, she insisted. Despite her protestations that her health and low spirits had negatively affected her appetite and that she had adopted no formal position against eating, however, the authorities proceeded with force-feeding.

She later wrote:

For three weeks I was the only suffragist prisoner in Holloway, but I really did not see any of the other suffragists for five weeks. During this time I was forcibly fed 15 times

– for 8 days, not because I had adopted the hunger strike, but because owing to my state of health I could eat only very little.

When I had been alone in prison two or three weeks, it was noticed that my weight was going down very much. Dr. Sullivan watched me for a few days and saw how very little I was eating. I tried to eat, for I had the horror always in my mind that they would forcibly feed me, but I was really too ill to eat. On 29 February, the Home Office specialist came down and saw me. He apparently told Dr. Sullivan that they would have to forcibly feed me. That night the matron came to me and tried to get me to eat, with some Brand's Essence[xvi] and tried to get me to take it. I did take some, but afterwards was sick. The next day the doctor came and said they would have to forcibly feed me.

By June, however, Davison conceded she had actively adopted the hunger strike. Other suffragettes had arrived by this time and perhaps she felt morally compelled to join them in their fast. It is also possible she felt that if she were going to be force-fed in either case, she might as well declare herself on strike. In the early days her spirits remained high. She and her comrades each wrote poems that were later collated in an anthology called *Holloway Jingles*. Davison's contribution, which invoked John Bunyan's *Pilgrim's Progress*, was written on 28 April 1912.[31]

---

xvi   An essence of chicken invented in 1820 by royal chef Henderson William Brand to try to revive the ailing King George IV.

L'ENVOI

Stepping onwards, oh my comrades!
Marching fearless through the darkness,
Marching fearless through the prisons,
With the torch of freedom guiding!

See the face of each is glowing,
Gleaming with the love of freedom;
Gleaming with a selfless triumph,
In the cause of human progress!

Like the pilgrim in the valley,
Enemies may oft assail us,
Enemies may close around us,
Tyrants, hunger, horror, brute-force.

But the glorious dawn is breaking,
Freedom's beauty sheds her radiance;
Freedom's clarion call is sounding,
Rousing all the world to wisdom.

Later, after her release, she wrote a full report about being examined by two doctors, one of whom was her friend, Charles
Mansell Moullin, whose wife Edith was an active suffragette
and fellow comrade. Davison wrote a bleak description of
the forcible feeding:

As it [the tube] passed down behind the throat a feeling

Portrait of Emily Wilding Davison, signed with her childhood nickname 'Pem'.
© THE WOMEN'S LIBRARY, LSE LIBRARY

Emily Wilding Davison's graduation portrait, 1908. She gained a Bachelor of Arts in modern languages from the University of London.

Portrait of Emily Wilding Davison wearing a portcullis-shaped 'prisoner's brooch' and another suffragette medal.

The information bureau of the Women's Social and Political Union (the suffragette organisation led by Emmeline Pankhurst). Emily Wilding Davison visited the offices, but was ostracised by the WSPU after she began to undertake militant missions without official instructions. © THE WOMEN'S LIBRARY, LSE LIBRARY

Davison's return train ticket from Epsom to Victoria Station on 4 June 1913, the day of the Epsom Derby. Some commentators have pointed to it to support the theory that she did not plan to collide with the King's horse, but instead wanted to return home that fateful day. © THE WOMEN'S LIBRARY, LSE LIBRARY

The aftermath of the suffragette's dramatic collision with King George V's horse Anmer at Epsom Derby on 4 June 1913. © THE WOMEN'S LIBRARY, LSE LIBRARY

The front page of British tabloid the *Daily Sketch*, the day after Emily Wilding Davison's death, 9 June 1913.

The front page of WSPU newspaper *The Suffragette* on 13 June 1913, the day before her public funeral.

Emily Wilding Davison's public funeral at St George's, Bloomsbury,
14 June 1913. © THE WOMEN'S LIBRARY, LSE LIBRARY

Madonna lily carried at
Emily Davison's funeral —
by Agnes A. Kelly.
June 14th 1913.

A pressed Madonna lily from the martyr suffragette's funeral.
© THE WOMEN'S LIBRARY, LSE LIBRARY

of suffocation and sickness followed ... I naturally commenced to cough, choke and retch.

This happened in every occasion. The result was that
the tube 'kinked ... It was very much more trying to be
fed by the junior dr [sic] as he was so unskillful and at
first made jeering remarks, which later however after a day
or two he did not indulge in ... When the job was over
whilst I was still retching the wardresses untied me and
threw me on to my bed, then left me at once and shut
the door. I was finally too exhausted and overcome to do
anything but lie like a loaf for some time, often retching
and coughing for an hour or so afterwards.

Davison's defiance in the face of such barbarity is notable.
Even the doctors commented on her energetic struggles
against forcible feeding. On one occasion, she recalled that the
senior doctor remarked, 'Miss Davison, you are determined'.

I replied in the brief interval as the tube was out: 'I am!'
He took it for granted that he knew I was choking up the
tube on purpose. As a matter of fact the action was natural
and involuntary but I always helped it as much as I could.

She noted that when she wriggled violently and 'looked specially suffocated' during forcible feeding, the doctors quickly
removed the rubber tubing.

I wondered ... when that happened if they had put it in

the wrong passage and what would result. When it went down the [wrong] place the feeling of retching and suffocation was unbearable. The Dr [sic] would often tell me to 'swallow', which I of course did not do. Instead I was glad to be sick, which often happened, and the rejected fluid went in the Dr's hands to his disgust and my satisfaction.

Subjected to such treatment, and drained from the hunger strike and perpetual struggle, some suffragettes consequently suffered severe trauma and mental agitation. Emmeline Pethick-Lawrence was, from her husband Frederick's observation, 'heading straight for a nervous breakdown', when in prison in 1906. Against her will, therefore, he paid her bail and retrieved her from jail, believing 'It was an imperative that she should be got out of prison without delay.'

Davison was in danger of slipping into the same psychological decline. She had been on her own for the majority of her prison stay, without the comfort of, or solidarity from, her usual band of fellow comrades. It was an extraordinarily lonely period of her life. Alongside the struggles with prison guards and traumatic incidents of forcible feeding, one of the overriding irritants of prison life was the boredom it entailed. Davison later jotted down, in a note entitled 'A Brief Record of My Life in Prison':

Deadly monotony when I went in, followed by the time when I could not eat and was forcibly fed, another period of blissful communication, this time followed by a hunger strike for the sake of my comrade…, not myself and another time of weary waiting, winding up with a glorious battle for freedom.

Like some of her comrades before her, she was pushed to psychological breaking point. Fed up with the brutal treatment of prison staff against the suffragettes, she decided a hard-hitting gesture was required. The sentiment that revolved in her mind, she later said, was that 'one big tragedy may save many others'. It was to be the most personally reckless act of any suffragette to date. Her fledgling spirit of martyrdom was about to take flight.

CHAPTER 8

A NEAR BRUSH WITH DEATH IN PRISON JUNE 1912

I n June 1912 Emily Wilding Davison suffered a near brush with death. The incident was self-willed and left her with broken vertebrae and a severe head injury. In an account written afterwards she described the series of events that led to the incident, and haunting thoughts that accompanied it.

She detailed the morale-sapping nature of solitary confinement, the terror of bear-like grown men trying to beat down a cell door, and the anguish prompted by hearing comrades' screams and groans echoing down the corridors. Her testimony not only vividly conjured the horror of her experience, it underscored her decision to attempt to end such treatment with the sacrifice of her life.

We resolved, as usual, to give every opportunity for

Constitutional pressure to win justice [first class 'political prisoner' status for Emily and her comrades]. For over a week we waited, every day asking for the Governor and demanding that we should be transferred to the first division, clearly warning him that if all other methods failed we should adopt the hunger strike. The day before we did this we gave him a twenty-four hours' ultimatum, and then began our fight, strictly to time.

On Wednesday, June 19th, from 10 a.m. onwards, we were kept in solitary confinement. On Saturday morning we decided that most of us would barricade our cells after they had been cleared out. At ten o'clock on the Saturday a regular siege took place in Holloway. On all sides one heard crowbars, blocks, and wedges being used; men battering on doors with all their might. The barricading was always followed by the sounds of human struggle, suppressed cries of the victims, groans, and other horrible sounds. These sounds came nearer and nearer in my direction. My turn came. I fought like a demon at my door, which was forced open with crowbars till at last enough room was made for one of the besiegers to get in. He pulled open the door, and in came wardresses and a doctor. I protested loudly that I would not be fed by the junior doctor, and tried to dart out into the passage; then I was seized by about five wardresses, bound into the chair, still protesting; and they accomplished their purpose. They threw me on my bed, and at once locked the door and went off to the next victim.

I lay like a log for some time. When I did recover a

little, I got up and smashed out the remaining panes of my window, then lay down again until I was able to get out into the corridor. In my mind was the thought that some desperate protest must be made to put a stop to the hideous torture which was now our lot. Therefore, as soon as I got out I climbed on to the railing and threw myself out on to the wire netting, a distance of between 20 and 30 feet. The idea in my mind was 'one big tragedy may save many others'; but the netting prevented any severe injury. The wardress in charge ran forward in horror. She tried to get me off the netting and whistled for help. Three others came and tried their best to induce me to go into my cell. I refused.

After a time their suspicions were allayed, and the matron came through into the ward to visit some of the prisoners; while she was there the wardresses relaxed their watch, and I began to look again. I realised that my best means of carrying out my purpose was the iron staircase. When a good moment came, quite deliberately I walked upstairs and threw myself from the top, as I meant, on to the iron staircase. If I had been successful I should un- doubtedly have been killed, as it was a clear drop of 30 to 40 feet. But I caught once more on the edge of the netting. A wardress ran to me, expostulating, and called on two of my comrades to try and stop me. As she spoke I realised that there was only once chance left, and was to hurl myself with the greatest force I could summon from the netting on to the staircase, a drop of about 10 feet. I heard someone saying, 'No surrender!' and threw myself forward on my head with all my might. I know nothing more except a fearful thud on my head.

When I recovered consciousness, it was to a sense of acute agony. Voices were buzzing around me; in the distance someone said, 'Fetch the doctor.' Someone tried to move me, and I called out, 'Oh, don't!'. Then the doctor came, and asked for me to be moved to a cell close by. They lifted me as gently as possible, but the agony was intense. It was all I could do to keep from screaming. And then I was placed on the cell bed. After a moment the doctor examined me, moving me as little as possible. He asked me to go to the hospital, but I begged him to leave me there – which he did. I also managed to say, 'For heaven's sake, don't feed me, because I shall fight.' I was therefore left very quietly, and they brought me some water, and did all they could for me.

The first night was one of misery, as I had to lie on my back, although it hurt me to do so. There was no sleep. Next day I at once demanded that the Governor should allow me to have my own doctor to examine me. I said, 'If you feed me before examination, it will be at your own risk.' The Governor asked me why I had done my deed, and I told him I thought that one big tragedy would save the others. His hand trembled, and he promised that he would see into the matter.

I was left alone until about two o'clock, when a specialist came in with the prison doctors. He thoroughly examined me, and seemed very much struck with my injuries.

Afterwards Dr. Sullivan confessed to me that he thought I had had the most extraordinary escape. To my amazement, the doctors came to forcibly feed me that afternoon. The operation, throughout which I struggled, caused me such agony that I begged the three comrades who were released that afternoon to let friends know outside what was being done.

After the doctor's visit, the regular routine of forcible feeding continued. Whether the prison authorities thought Davison strong enough to withstand it, or simply concluded that she desperately needed nourishment, is difficult to ascertain, but the attempt came at her 'amazement'. She wrote:

> I had clearly warned them that whatever happened I should resist. I was so little expecting them that I was quietly lying in bed, and so quickly did they come on me that I had no time to get out of bed. I cried out saying: 'You surely are not such brutes as to feed me by force when I am so ill!!' They merely answered by … pinning me down to the bed. All the time I suffered the greatest agony from my aching head and back but there was no pity shown.

The emotional effects of the practice resonate in all Davison's accounts of force-feeding, but this was the only instance in which she admitted on paper: 'I cried at, and after, the operation.'

Physically she continued to suffer 'torture with my head and back' following the staircase incident. As she lay in recovery, she was forcibly fed again the next day. She elaborated further on the tactics employed to catch her unawares:

> The custom was to try and rush in on me to surprise me in bed. As a result the minute I heard the key in the door I would jump out of bed in spite of pain and rush to hold on to the shelf ... Sometimes, to avoid them, I would get out, put my shoes on and stand in the cold to avoid being surprised – I then had a tussle with the wardresses who would finally bang me into the hardwood chair, into which no cushion was put to save my back. I cried out repeatedly that my back was being hurt when they would tell me that I should not struggle. On one occasion the cloth round my neck was tied so tight that I thought I should be choked – as the last stage of my struggle always was bending forward low to avoid the doctor the misery and pain I suffered can be well guessed.

Davison explained she suffered acute indigestion from the amount of liquid poured down her throat too. She vomited after each force-feeding on the sixth day after the staircase incident. The pain of the practice twice a day was intolerable, so she sought to negotiate with the prison doctor:

> I told him about the indigestion, and asked him either to give me less each time, or only to feed me once a day. He said that others had been making similar complaints and that he was going to try the effect of only feeding us once a day

on more concentrated diet. This he did on Wednesday and Thursday to our great relief. We told him that the mental relief was incalculable. All this time we had been in close confinement in our cells, but owing to the remarks of several of our women, notably the nurse Miss Hudson, those who were strong enough were allowed about an hour's exercise for the first time on Wednesday – I was of course in bed.

Her report also contained details of the injuries she had suffered in her fall.

Meantime nothing was being done to make my condition better. My head was dressed on Sunday [four days after the staircase incident]. Nothing further was done to it. By the examination I knew that besides the two injuries to my head the seventh cervicle vertebra was injured, and another at the base of the spine. They seemed very much worried about my right shoulder blade. The sacrum bone was also injured, not to mention the many bruises all over my arms and back. All the vertebrae at the back of the head are very painful, and it is torture to turn.

On Thursday Dr. Sullivan examined me fairly carefully, and asked me to be weighed. I consented, and found that I had lost 4lbs. at least since the Friday when I threw myself over … On the Thursday evening after the one forcible feeding operation, the doctor opened my cell door and announced the medical inspector. He walked in, and was followed by a gentleman who gave his name as Dr. Craig.

The psychiatric examination was to prove a dangerous moment for Davison. The authorities believed, or at least purported to believe, that the actions and high-spiritedness of the imprisoned suffragettes likely pointed to mental imbalances. If signed off as clinically insane by a medical professional, a prisoner could be locked up indefinitely in the harsh conditions of the asylums that abounded at the turn of the twentieth century. Bound in a straitjacket, a prisoner would not be able to effect even mild vandalism in a cell.

Although an extreme solution, it was nonetheless one way to eliminate problematic members of society from causing further trouble. The prospect of being locked up in a criminal psychiatric institution loomed large over the incarcerated suffragettes, an added insult to the egregious physical trauma they suffered while in prison. A sentence could be extended indefinitely if such a prisoner was deemed 'dangerous'.

Mary Richardson was one suffragette who faced the prospect of being declared mentally ill.[32] After vandalising her cell in protest against being forced to give her fingerprints for a fourth time, she refused to speak to the prison doctor when he asked her to declare the day of the week and the name of her grandmother. Menacingly, the doctor asked her: 'Do you think the state of this cell is evidence of a sane mind?' She quickly realised the danger she was in and answered the questions properly, defending her sanity and explaining the reasons behind her violent protest. The doctor and assembled group of prison warders decided to let her remain in jail, rather than an asylum. She later wrote of the experience:

I sank back on my hard pillow, every ounce of my energy spent. Vaguely, uncertainly I felt that everything was over with me. I was lost in some labyrinth of ingenious cruelty. I kept remembering the words of a noble Lord who in a speech had said of me, 'That woman, Mary Richardson, is a most dangerous type of criminal lunatic.'

As the three doctors entered her cell, Davison's mental state was also to be assessed. The psychiatric examinations had been used against some of her comrades as a tool of terror to pressure them into submission. Given she had hurled herself down an iron staircase, however, it may well have seemed remiss not to question her purpose and mental welfare. She wrote:

On Thursday afternoon, Dr. Sullivan brought in 'the medical inspector'. Dr. Sullivan, who was followed by a third doctor, whose name was given me as Dr. Craig. I surmised that he was a mental specialist, and have since ascertained that this was right. He was very pleasant and courteous. The three doctors sat down in my cell and a long examination and cross-examination followed. I was questioned as to my state of health, whether I had any delusions, fears and fancies.

The three of them sat down in my cell, and subjected me to a long examination and cross-examination. I calmly gave them all the information that I could, and seemed thoroughly to satisfy any doubts they had as to my sanity. In the course of the examination I believe I made them realise what a disgrace it was to England, and the medical profession, that such torture as forcible feeding should have been resorted to rather than granting justice to women. They weakly put forward the argument that their only mission was to save life, but could not deny that mental torture was hardly the safest way of doing so. I also made them realise that we women set this great cause of ours before everything else in the world; or, as I put it to them, the cause of human progress was above that of any possible material consideration. Dr. Craig thoroughly examined all my injuries, seemed greatly impressed by them, and when he shook hands with me said, 'Don't do any more for your cause; you have done more than enough.'

On the Friday morning, Dr. Sullivan examined me again, and told me that I should probably be released that day later on. He said he would not trouble me with the forcible feeding, if when I was released I would take some food before going out. I said, 'Oh no; I absolutely refuse to take any food within the prison walls.' He therefore decided that he must forcibly feed me again, for the ninth time – which was done.

All that day I got no chance of letting my comrades know that I should be released, which they would have been glad of, because they were all very anxious that I should be. In the afternoon the doctor came and officially announced my release, said that all packing must be done for me, and asked me if, when I was in the cab, I would take some Brand's Essence. He said that the tin 'should not be opened until I was outside, so that I should know it was not contaminated by the Home Secretary.' I smiled and told him that I was willing to take anything once I was outside the walls.

By 6 o'clock I was quite ready. Then the wardresses who saw me go said they were very glad and hoped I would not come again. I was not able to say 'goodbye' to my dear comrades, whom I hated leaving. The old porter at the gate, when he asked for my name, said, 'Well, I am glad to see you are out at last' – and I went forth into freedom.

Emily was liberated once again. She had gone into Holloway Prison weighing 9st. 12 ½ lbs. On her release, she was down to 7st. 8 ½ lbs. She wrote at the end of one of her reports, dated 8 July: 'I am still in bed recovering, careful nursing.' Physically, she never fully recovered from the injuries sustained on the iron staircase.

CHAPTER 9

'TO LAY DOWN LIFE FOR FRIENDS ... THAT IS GLORIOUS' JUNE 1912–JUNE 1913

fter her release from prison, Davison went to recuperate at the Penn Gaskells' house. The journey there from Holloway Prison exhausted her and she limped to bed as soon as she arrived. Her injuries were severe and her recovery slow. During the days she spent with her activist friends, she talked often of her conviction that a life had to be given to achieve women's enfranchisement.

Eleanor Penn Gaskell was taken aback by Davison's fervour and obsession with the idea. She argued that even if Davison were right, that life should not be hers. Echoing the doctor who had been moved by the suffragette's commitment to her cause, Penn Gaskell told her friend that she had already done enough for the cause. Unrelenting, however, Davison would respond to this protest with the repeated refrain: 'Why not I as well as another?'[33] While Davison's friends attempted to reason with her and made emotional appeals, Emmeline and Christabel Pankhurst took a colder approach to their rebellious colleague. They had begun to view her as a liability rather than an asset to the movement. They terminated her employment at the WSPU office and actively began to distance themselves from her. They would not even publish her account of her Holloway incident in *The Suffragette*. After her death, at which point they felt she could be safely extolled as a heroine and martyr to the cause, their sentiments changed and the account was duly printed in full.

Sylvia later wrote that the WSPU had been displeased by Davison's unauthorised arson of postboxes and other free-lancing actions, fearing it would turn public opinion against their cause.

The organisation leadership had wanted 'to discourage [Davison] in such tendencies ... She was condemned and os-tracised as a self-willed person who persisted in acting upon her own initiative without waiting for official instructions.'[34] It was not only the public, and elements of the government previously sympathetic to the cause, that the rebels' arson campaign repelled: it was some members of the WSPU itself. In 1912 a flurry of members quit the Union in protest and joined the NUWSS instead.

Davison was less vocal about her belief in the need for the sacrifice of a life to advance women's suffrage in front of her mother. Although close, the pair tended not to discuss the younger woman's activism. Margaret could not bear to hear her daughter talk about hunger strikes or the militant acts that would land her yet again in prison. They agreed, therefore, that any respite that the suffragette enjoyed at home in Longhorsley should entail rest from the cause – with no discussion of the activities or philosophy around it. However, when visitors came to see Davison, she would update them in whispering tones out of earshot, or so she thought, of her mother. Margaret later said: 'She could not help talking about it, and when the doctor came, or the Catholic priest, with whom she was friends, I would hear her in another room discussing it.'

Outside her mother's home, Davison took time to evangelise in Morpeth, often from an open car in the market-place.[35] Not all her acts in the name of the cause were set-piece heroics and she engaged with enthusiasm in the task of proselytising in public about the women's rights movement. It is notable that she did not become well known for her speaking skills, however, unlike Annie Kenney, the articulate mill girl from Saddleworth, who became a poster child of the movement.

Nor was Davison's connection to the suffragettes anchored solely in London where the leading activists tended to amass. She was closely aligned to a group of local activists in the north-east. One of these, Norah Balls, later a respected historian, lecturer and magistrate, recalled visiting Davison and her mother Margaret.

'Mother Davison, as we used to call her, had a cottage at

Longhorsely [sic], and we used to go there on our bikes for a lovely country tea on Sunday afternoons,' she said. Like Davison, Balls herself took part in daring suffragette missions, including in 1914 starting a fire in Gosforth House, since renamed Brandling House, a Grade II listed hall in Newcastle upon Tyne.[36]

In the second half of 1912, the toll on Davison's health from starvation and violent resistance against prison authorities became increasingly apparent. Her doctor warned her in certain terms that although of a naturally strong constitution, the strain she leveraged on her body was unsustainable in the long term. She little heeded the cautionary advice and, after recovering her energy, continued to dash around the region giving speeches and lectures to grassroots activists within the WSPU.

She was a prolific writer, a pastime that served the dual purpose of earning her a modest income as well as providing a cathartic outlet for her thoughts. She was a keen critic of art and theatre and also wrote essays and letters to newspapers to advance the cause without risk of injury or imprisonment. It is thought that she worked in the information bureau of the WSPU before she was ostracised from the central command by the organisation's leadership. How much money she earned from her written endeavours is unclear and her financial affairs in general remain opaque. It is possible she was given money by her mother or the movement's wealthy donors, and that she lodged for free with better-off comrades from time to time.

In August 1912, Davison drafted a letter to the editor of a Canadian newspaper, the *Western Home Monthly*, following a visit by the Canadian Prime Minister to Britain. In the letter she discussed militancy in the context of publicity. She raged at a press boycott on the women's suffrage movement and how she felt the print media twisted the suffragettes' acts of militancy, citing, perhaps unwisely, the example of her friend, Mary Leigh, setting alight theatre curtains in Dublin. 'The press stories of militant actions by suffragettes are one of the hardest things we have to fight,' Davison wrote.

She continued to draft similar letters for publication as the autumn arrived. In September she wrote to the *Newcastle Journal* and complained about force-feeding: 'If our nation could only realise the degradation, the unspeakable misery which it involves to the helpless prisoner, it could not allow such re-enactment of mediaeval barbarity to be carried on.' In another letter, this time to the *Newcastle Chronicle*, she explained the rationale and aims of militancy. It was addressed to 'Mary', a woman who had complained in an earlier issue of the paper that the militancy of the WSPU suffragettes meant that many women needed courage just to openly admit they supported the concept of women's suffrage.

Davison's retort to this assertion was that the advancement of the cause called for sacrifice, but that 'the sacrifice varies according to circumstance. It may be loss of livelihood, position, wealth, friends, relatives and, not least common, loss of health or even possibly life.' She made clear in no uncertain terms that such sacrifices are not 'lightly made', but at the same time alluded to her belief that it was the duty of all women to struggle for the cause, to whatever degree they could.

She revealed her own sense of loss from her militancy in the telling remark: 'In all this, no mention of the personal shrinking a woman feels as a matter of certainty after being thrust into publicity.' Davison gave up a great deal to commit herself wholly to the cause. She lived out her life in the public domain and threw herself dauntlessly into a cycle of militant acts, prison sentences, hunger strikes and recovery. Her friends were her comrades – most other acquaintances from her earlier life abandoned the dangerous firebrand activist. She had no children, never married and enjoyed no romantic life at all, so far as documented evidence suggests.

In the same notebook as she recorded her letters to the press, Davison considered the nature of militancy and grappled with the central question of whether it was the best means by which the vote could be won. Political enfranchisement for women was, to her mind, the crucial and most urgent target. It was not just an end, but the means by which other improvements to women's lives could be won. The vote would afford women political leverage to influence legislation about their wages, their role in marriage and their rights following divorce.

In a letter to the *Morning Advertiser* Davison set out her argument for equal pay for, and attitudes towards, married women. From her letters it is clear that, while she pursued militant methods, she did not disregard peaceful means of calling for constitutional change as well. Davison considered the tactics complementary.

In October 1912, for example, she and fellow activist Laura Ainsworth made a deputation to Thomas Burt MP in Newcastle to obtain his views on the Franchise Reform Bill. According to the *Morpeth Herald*, 'Mr Burt intimated that he would vote for amendments to give the suffrage to women. Asked if he would bring pressure to bear on the Prime Minister to induce him to embody woman suffrage in the Bill, Mr Burt's answer was in the negative.'[37]

She was also committed to using the written word to explain and defend the suffragettes' militancy, and to put right misguided assumptions and malicious assertions. In another letter to the *Morning Advertiser* in 1911, she said:

It is perfectly true that the right way to get grievances redressed is to appeal to the institutions appointed for that purpose. But what is to be done if the appointed institutions fail to take notice of the grievance, although reiterated often and strongly during, say, 50 years? Is it right to continue to sit down under the grievance? Is it not indeed criminal and cowardly? It is an axiom of politics that those who accept tyranny are worthy of tyranny, and further that rebellion against tyrants is obedience to God!...

No reform was ever won in this country without a very great deal of effort. It is impossible to avoid remarking that in the case of the women's agitation the violence done so far has been mild compared to the men's agitation in past days,

*especially in 1832, 1867, and during this strike year of 1911,
and the resulting inconvenience has been suffered by the
women themselves and not the public, as in the men's cases.*[38]

Letters like these were among Davison's more nuanced,
well-reasoned writing. Other items in her archive were less
persuasive or cogently argued. In all, despite her natural intelligence, she was not an intellectual. Nonetheless, most of
her writing affords a glimpse of her personality and attitudes.

A piece about alleged corruption in the Metropolitan
Police, entitled 'London equals New York', revealed her
poor opinion of the police, for example. It was based upon a
speech she heard ex-Inspector John Syme give in Trafalgar
Square. Syme had been dismissed from the police service
in 1910 for insubordination, and carried on a feud with the
police for the next thirty years, which several times landed
him in prison for criminal libel.

She wrote:

A Sunday afternoon one of the most interesting meetings
in the Cause of Progress was held in Trafalgar Square
when a brave man, Ex-Inspector Syme, exposed to the
'British Public' the terrible system of corrupt officialdom
which exists in the Metropolitan Police force today. To
an audience mainly composed of the thoughtful citizen
which forms the backbone of the country, he un-folded a
ghastly tale which is sucking the very life-blood out of the
police-force...

She went on to repeat his claim that cases against innocents were being manufactured, and added:

> The rank and file of the force themselves dare not protest against this juggernaut ... for if they dare to fit their voices in protest (as some have done) they were victimised, degraded and assaulted by 'superior' officers, until in some cases young police men had been driven to committing suicide.

It was not surprising that Davison was, in the wake of her own experiences, prepared to believe the worst of the Metropolitan Police.

She also took a dim view of politicians. In 1912 Lloyd George, the Chancellor, led opposition to the Parliamentary Franchise (Women) Bill that had finally arrived in the Commons. On second reading the bill was defeated in a knife-edge vote, 222 votes to 208. Eighty Irish MPs had opposed it, fearing the bill would take up parliamentary time they wanted to see spent on the Home Rule Bill for Ireland.[39] Hatred of Lloyd George intensified among the suffragettes.

Months later in February 1913 an attack on his property occurred for which Davison was later named as the perpetrator, though the proof is inconclusive. A house that was under construction for the Chancellor was bombed. Most of the rooms in the half-built property in Walton Heath, Surrey, were destroyed by the explosives. It was Sylvia Pankhurst who named Davison as the culprit in her 1931 memoir: 'At 6 a.m. on 18 February, a bomb set by Emily Wilding Davison and accomplices wrecked five rooms of a partly-completed house that Lloyd George was having built near Walton Heath, Surrey.'

Little more is known about the incident, but a secret bombing campaign was later referenced by Edith Mansell Moullin, a close friend of Davison's, in a 1930 letter to another suffragette. Mansell Moullin, writing about a planned biography of Davison's life, asked her colleague whether she should '(as I do) ... leave out the bombs? Although one did actually blow a piece off the Coronation Chair!!'

Though the house had in the event been empty, the escapade would have marked an escalation in the degree of risk to human life that Davison was prepared to take. The explosives could have caused harm if there had been anyone in the building and moreover they presented a danger to those left to clear up the debris.

Whether or not she was behind the bombing of the Chancellor's house, Davison's capacity for violence had increased in that final year before her death.

On 30 November 1912 a woman, immediately identified by police as the by-then notorious suffragette, thought she espied Lloyd George at Aberdeen railway station. In an opportunistic attack, she ran at him and beat him viciously with a dog whip that happened to be to hand. The man she assaulted was not the Chancellor, however, but a local Baptist minister with an uncannily similar face who was seeing off his wife on a train. Davison was arrested for the attack on Rev. Forbes Jackson and gave her name as 'Mary Brown'.

Her pseudonym was the maiden name of her close friend, Mary Leigh.

In December 1912, Davison was tried at the Crown Terrace Baptist Church in Aberdeen for the offence. The judge she faced was unlikely to have been sympathetically predisposed to her cause; he had just suffered the indignity of having a shoe hurled at him by a suffragette who went by the name of Ms Locke.[xvii] She had been arrested on the same day as Davison for possessing explosive cork cartridges known as 'explosive bombs' which, when fired from a toy pistol, made a loud bang. Locke and two comrades were thought to have been plotting to hurl the corks onto a stage on which the Chancellor was speaking in the music hall in Aberdeen. The trio, to their surprise, were granted bail.[40] Their plan was condemned for having endangered the lives of the crowd, as the intended commotion could have prompted a crush.

Confusion has arisen in intervening years about whether Davison was the genuine culprit in the crime, as she disputed the charge against her. However, contemporary press reports help unravel the puzzle: she accepted her involvement in the incident but not its description under the law. She was charged with assaulting the Baptist minister, but argued she should have been charged with attacking Lloyd George. Furthermore, she declared her rejection of the court's jurisdiction and refused to partake in the trial. It was Davison's long-standing contention, set out in several of her essays and

xvii   A pseudonym used by Olive Wharry. At other times she went by the name Phyllis North.

letters of newspapers, that the UK's judicial system could not be truly just until women sat on juries.

Such a violent assault did seem out of character for the suffragette, however, and it was a strange coincidence that she had been carrying a whip. Nonetheless, by this time Davison was increasingly enveloped in her obsession with the cause and isolated from less hardline activists who might have dampened her fervour. The harm her actions caused to others, albeit often indirectly, was often a blind spot. She is said to have claimed, for example, after starting a fire in a West End theatre, 'There was no danger to the public at all, for the attempt was made when the theatre was nearly emptied.' A cavalier attitude and reckless approach characterised her public persona and won her heavy criticism in the press.

While sometimes naïve or wilfully obtuse about the risks attendant to her behaviour, Davison appeared later to regret the Aberdeen attack on an innocent man. Some years later she cut out and kept his obituary in *The Times*, which improbably blamed her for his death. The ragged cutting was said to have been found on her after her collision at the Derby.

It is likely that the particular circumstances that led the suffragettes to encircle the train station in Aberdeen that autumn day in 1912 had riled Davison to a new, heightened degree. It is said that they had hoped to confront Lloyd George about their rough treatment by the Aberdeen Shore Porters, who had been drafted in to top up the politician's security detail. The porters were accused of causing serious injury.[41]

Contemporary press reports stated that, mid-morning, a suffragette leader had spied the reverend stepping from a carriage on a train about to depart for Caledonia and identified him with a cry as Lloyd George. Jackson was said to have protested he was not the Liberal politician, but was accused by the woman of attempting to disguise his true self. A man working for the Caledonian Railway allegedly apprehended the woman swiping violently at the man's face with a whip and a struggle ensued.[42] Other reports told that she beat him with her hands rather than any object.

The legal charge, according to a report in the *Aberdeen Daily Journal*,[xviii] stated:

> On 30th November, within the Joint Station, in a compartment of a railway carriage forming part of a Caledonian train, accused assaulted the Rev. Forbes Jackson ... by striking him of the head and shoulders with a whip and seizing him by the collar of the coat and shaking and jostling him about, and conducted herself in a lawless and disorderly manner, and committed a breach of the peace.

The *Aberdeen Daily Journal* for Tuesday 3 December[43] gave a vivid report of the court hearing.

> There was a large crowd of the general public waiting in the street, and the great majority were unable to secure

---

xviii   Unusually for the time, the newspaper contained a female reporter in its newsroom: Caroline Phillips, who was secretary of the Aberdeen WSPU.

admission to the Police Court. Mr Jackson arrived a minute after ten o'clock. The reverend gentleman bears a distinct, if not altogether striking resemblance to Mr Lloyd George. What people came to see, however, was the lady in the case. After the usual preliminaries Baillie Robertson was read to proceed. It was half past ten when the bar officer cried: 'Mary Browne alias Emily Wilding Davison.'

The door swung open, and the suffragette entered. She was clad in a heavy grey overcoat, with green hat and sported a big coloured party badge. A small armful of newspapers showed how she had been engaged. She walked jauntily into the court, did not deign to look towards the bench, but turned her attention to the 'gallery'. She smiled to someone and lifted her hand in a gay salute. Then and only then did she face the Baillie.[xix] The Clerk of the Court commenced to read the charge and had got no further than the accused's name when she brought him to a halt with a peremptory demand – 'What is that you are saying?'

She went on:

I tell you sir, I deny entirely the jurisdiction of this court. I entirely deny that a court composed of men only has any right to deal with the case of a woman, because by Magna Carta we have the right to be tried by our peers, and peers

---

xix   A Scottish judge.

mean women as well as men. I deny the jurisdiction of this court.

Davison demanded time to amass witnesses and the hearing was postponed for several days. By the time the court convened again, public interest in the case was high. Many 'fashionably attired ladies' were anxious to gain admission and women packed out the gallery.

The Reverend Jackson proceeded to give testimony about how he had been leapt upon in a railway carriage while waving off his wife on the train. According to the *Aberdeen Daily Journal*, he said:

> This lady came along who I thought was an ordinary passenger. And without any explanation she cried 'You traitor! You traitor!'. There came quite a rain of blows, nothing serious in the sense of physical injury, the whip being quite a light thing, I suppose more a symbol than a weapon.

He said, according to another contemporary press report:[44]

> A little after that I came back. The police had taken her into a lobby. I went up to the office, and to my astonishment she landed me a very clever quick blow on the left jaw with her clenched fist. That was the conclusion of the whole matter so far as I was concerned.

Asked whether it was a severe blow, he replied to laughter:

'Well, it was a woman's blow.' Quizzed further as to whether she had hurt him with the whip, leaving marks, he said: 'Well, no'. The blows by her fists, rapidly administered, numbered at least half a dozen, he estimated.

While the minister accepted that Davison bore him no personal grudge, he told her: 'I am quite satisfied that you had, and have still, a bias of a very evil kind against the man you thought I was.' He was determined to pursue the case. Miss Fussell, an organiser of the Aberdeen WSPU, had called on him in the immediate aftermath of the incident to accept an apology from Davison, but he had declined.

In the court Davison attempted to highlight the minister's churlishness, pointing to a similar incident in the Commons that had been resolved by an apology. Winston Churchill had openly mocked Ronald McNeill, an Irish MP, by waving a white handkerchief at him, prompting the target to retaliate by hurling a small bound order book at the First Lord of the Admiralty, which was said to have hit him in the head. Churchill apologised and that was an end to the matter.[45]

Davison ended the trial with a political address, which the judge attempted to close down. Before she could be halted, she declared: 'At Kirkcaldy when a woman asked Mr Lloyd George to do justice to women he said "Don't be a fool and idiot", whereas in Aberdeen when a student said "Don't forget the ladies" he bowed and smiled. That was the different, unfair way in which women were treated over that question.'

A guilty sentence was handed down, sparking a commotion in the public gallery among Davison's comrades. She shouted 'No surrender!' before she was led away to a cell. She was sentenced to ten days in prison for assault, but undertook a hunger strike and was released after four days.

In the aftermath of the attack and brief prison term, Davison found herself at a loss. At this time she had no fixed income, and relations with the Union meant employment there was not an option. She could not reconcile close association with the Union and being under their administration with her autonomy as a 'freelance' activist. Nor were the Pankhursts keen to risk the unpredictable rebel disturbing their plans at the WSPU headquarters.

Davison took a trip, therefore, to France, where she stayed with her sister who lived in Dunkirk. Many of her siblings had moved abroad – her full brother Alfred got as far as Vancouver, Canada, where he lived until his death in 1918 from pneumonia. Letitia had married a Frenchman in 1895 and crossed the English Channel.[46] Davison was thrilled to spend time with her sister and young nephew and niece. She styled herself the children's devoted 'Auntie Pem' and took an interest both in their games and their studies. In an echo of her mother's role at the helm of a bakery in Longhorsley, she also delighted to give the infants baked treats. During this visit she took the children to the circus and the fair and, given all she had endured in the year beforehand, surprised her family with her liveliness and gaiety.

Scholars agree that it was likely around this time that

Davison wrote her undated essay 'A Militant on May Day', in which she declared: 'For the first time in my life I have taken part in a May Day demonstration as a militant suffragist.' She went on to describe her joy at being among a crowd of socialists in Hyde Park on the festival day. The offices of the WSPU had just been raided, and she was deeply moved by the support of the socialists marching to the park on behalf of the Union. There was also a hint of scorn detectable in her description of nervous middle-class observers dawdling outside the park, who were, to her mind, at odds with the courageous and energetic socialists. She wrote:

> Socialism represents the day of Liberty, Fraternity and Equality, when wars shall cease, when each man and woman shall labour and receive the fruits of their labours, when little children shall grow up in decent environments with full opportunities, when England and her sister-nations too shall be indeed 'merry'. I came away from this May Day Demonstration with a glimpse of the vision of the future: 'Behold I make all things new!'

Davison's admiration for the socialist movement was clear. She became an executive of the Workers' Educational Association during this period and was also an active member of the Central Labour College. While the NUWSS asked its activists to focus only on women gaining the vote, the WSPU was relaxed about its members lobbying for other causes. For Davison, workers' rights could not be separated from women's suffrage. It was, she believed, an extension of a crippling patriarchy that kept both the working poor and women oppressed.

Her loyalties ranged from God and the cause of women's suffrage to socialism and friendship. The last of these values she extended most freely and passionately to Mary Leigh. In December 1912, Davison gave her fellow suffragette a book of poetry in which she had underlined significant passages. Using the pseudo-military salutations the suffragettes favoured, she inscribed the book:

> With all Good Wishes for 'The institution of the dear love of comrades.'
> From: Comrade Davison
> To: Comrade Leigh
> Dec. 29, 1912

One particular poem that she marked out, by American poet Walt Whitman, appeared to chime precisely with Davison's attitude:

> I HEAR it is charged against me that I sought to destroy
>   institutions;
> But really I am neither for nor against institutions,
> (What indeed have I in common with them? – Or what
> with the destruction of them?)
> Only I will establish in the Mannahatta, and in every city
>   of These States, inland and seaboard

And in the fields and woods, and above every keel little
    or large, that dents the water,
  Without edifices, or rules, or trustees, or any argument,
    The institution of the dear love of comrades.

The last line was underlined three times by Davison. It was not the only one. Other lines in poems by Whitman were marked, some of which appear, in hindsight, to have presaged her death. In light of her earlier attempted sacrifice in Holloway Prison at the well of the iron staircase, and the incident at the Derby yet to come, lines such as these can be read through the prism of martyrdom:

And as to you Death, and you bitter hug of mortality, it is
idle to try to alarm me

Elsewhere in the anthology, she marked out this stanza from Whitman's poem 'So Long':

Dear friend, whoever you are, here, take this kiss,
I give it especially to you – Do not forget me,
I feel like one who has done his work – I progress on,
The unknown sphere, more real than I dreamed, more
direct, darts awakening rays about me – So long!
Remember my words – I love you – I depart from
materials, I am as one disembodied, triumphant, dead.

It was the strongest platonic bond Davison enjoyed in her life.

Whether any deeper romantic sentiments were exchanged between her and Leigh, or harboured on one side, it is impossible to know. The notion that suffragettes were fuelled by sexual repression was a common insult hurled at the movement by high-profile anti-suffrage campaigners. Female activists were also accused of being 'unwomanly' and 'unladylike', and of fighting against their supposedly natural state.

In an unpublished essay entitled 'Incendiarism', Davison explained her rationale for the arson campaign she waged in December 1911, and cited the unjust treatment of Leigh as her motivation for the militant activity. She made clear her anger and pain at Leigh being awarded what she felt was an unduly long, and spiteful, sentence in prison earlier that month. Leigh, for her part, also held Davison in clear affection, visiting her friend's grave annually after her death.

Davison had turned forty in October 1912. She had sacrificed the previous five years of her life, as well as her health and liberty, to the cause. However, her militancy and notoriety meant that even many of the most hardline suffragettes were keen to put public distance between themselves and the rebel activist. For the escalating militancy of the WSPU had been matched by a fall in its membership.

Millicent Fawcett, head of the peaceable suffrage organisation the NUWSS, said in 1912 that her organisation had grown to 30,000 subscribers. She meanwhile numbered the WSPU membership at 8,000. Other reports state that by 1914 the NUWSS had grown to 50,000 members, while the WSPU by that time had only 5,000.

Historian Sir Brian Harrison concluded: 'WSPU membership fees suggest that fewer new members were joining in each year between 1909 and 1914; after October 1913, perhaps to avoid advertising this fact, new members' fees were no longer published.'

Prominent WSPU activist Mary Richardson said years later: 'The actual front-line militants numbered only one thousand odd; and even this figure had dwindled after the "Cat and Mouse" Act had been introduced.'

This act, officially known as the Prisoners Temporary Discharge Act, was passed in March 1913. The Liberal government felt it had suffered enough humiliation at the hands of the wily suffragettes, who were viewed as winning the publicity war with their hunger strikes. It did not help the authorities that in 1913 a group of bishops had convened in London to condemn force-feeding. The new act aimed to minimise the use of force-feeding by releasing hunger-striking suffragettes 'on licence' once their weight plummeted to a level bordering on dangerous. Once the woman in question had recovered her strength, however, or if she committed another offence, she would be rounded up and re-imprisoned to serve the rest of her sentence.

Dubbed the 'Cat and Mouse' Act by the press for the way in which its tactics resembled a cat toying with his prey before devouring it, the act did not provide the desired effect on the behaviour of the suffragettes. It did, however, stem the negative publicity the authorities received. The dissidents were outraged by the government's guile, though they gained reprieve from the agony of force-feeding.

Davison was aware that to many old friends and acquaintances her militant actions had been unpalatable. In January 1913 when she was at Longhorsley with her mother, she wrote a letter to a friend she addressed only as 'Beloved old schoolfellow'. She admitted she feared her friend had abandoned her:

> *I was indeed glad to get your card, and to find that you were still willing to 'own me'! I had not heard from you for so long that I had almost come to the conclusion that you, like many others, had got to the pitch of thinking I was too militant.*

She explained that she was at home with her mother, 'who is glad to have me and to know that I am not too much battered' and proceeded to write candidly about her experiences of the past year:

> *The long imprisonment last year, and the terrible finale, did not, of course, do me much good, but somehow I come up smiling. This last four days' hunger strike in Aberdeen, of course, found out my weakness, and I have had some rheumatism in my neck and back, where I fell on that iron staircase. If it is wet or I am tired both parts ache, and I have bumps. My mother does not know this, thank goodness, and really, of course, I look and feel well ... At present I have no settled work here or in town. While here I busy myself writing my*

experiences and doing what I can to help my mother ... I wish
I could hear of some [work] though.

Short of money, and unwanted at WSPU headquarters,
Davison fired off a series of applications for writing work
in the spring of 1913. A friend wrote to the editor of the
Manchester Guardian on her behalf, imploring: 'She is
anxious to get some literary work, and will be extremely
grateful for any advice you can give her on the subject.' One
response to an application from the *Nursing Times* stated,
in a tone approaching disdainful: 'I suppose you realise
that writing about a cause is quite different from the hack
work you will have to do if you get on the ordinary papers?'
Other letters revealing her failure to secure work at this
time are scattered throughout her archive. A letter from
the Women's Tax Resistance League to Davison stated: 'In
reply to your letter of this morning, it was not a secretary we
required, but a junior shorthand typist. We therefore beg to
return your testimonials with thanks.'

It appears that disappointment about her prospects served
to stiffen her resolve to make a worthwhile gesture to further the cause. In September 1912, she had told the *Pall Mall
Gazette* that the staircase incident at Holloway had been a
deliberate attempt 'to commit suicide'. 'I did it deliberately and with all my power,' she wrote, 'because I felt that by
nothing but the sacrifice of human life would the nation be
brought to realise the horrible torture our women face. If I
had succeeded I am sure that forcible feeding could not in all

conscience have been resorted to again.' In 1913, in what was likely the last article she would ever write, she once again returned to the theme of martyrdom and making the ultimate sacrifice. On 28 May in the *Daily Sketch* there appeared what the suffragette paper *Votes for Women* later described as 'The Last Written Word of Emily Wilding Davison'. In the essay[xx] she made clear her view that the path on which she had set out in her direct action campaign led only to one destination. She wrote:

The true suffragette is an epitome of the determination of women to possess their own souls. The words of the Master are eternally true: 'What shall it profit a man if he gain the whole world and lose his own soul?' And it is the realisation of this ideal that is moving the most advanced of the feminists to stand out at all costs today.

...In the New Testament the Master reminded His followers that when the merchant had found the Pearl of Great Price, he sold all that he had in order to buy it. That is the parable of Militancy! It is that which the woman warriors are doing today. Some are truer warriors than others, but the perfect Amazon is she who will sacrifice all even unto this last to win the Pearl of Freedom for her sex.

Some of the beauteous pearls that women sell to obtain this freedom ... are the pearls of Friendship, Good Report, Love, and even Life itself ... Who will gainsay

---

xx   The full text is reproduced in Appendix 1.

that Friendship is one of the priceless jewels of life? ... Yet this pearl is sacrificed without a moment's hesitation by the true militant ... An even severer part of the price is the surrender of Good Report – one of the brightest and most precious of the gems in a woman's crown, as anyone can realise who knows how easily her fair fame is sullied ... Hence, to women, reputation is often as dear as life itself. Yet even this jewel has been sacrificed by the militant.

But a more soul-rending sacrifice even than that of friendship and of good report is demanded of the militant, that of the blood tie. 'She that loveth mother or father, sister or brother, husband or child, dearer than me cannot be my disciple,' saieth the terrible voice of freedom in accents that rend the very heart in twain.

'Cannot this cup of anguish be spared me?' cries the militant aloud in agony, yet immediately, as if in repentance for having so nearly lost the Priceless Pearl, in the words of all strivers after progress, she ejaculates: 'Nevertheless I will pay, even unto this price'; and in her writhing asks what further demand can be exacted from her.

The glorious and inscrutable Spirit of Liberty has but one further penalty within its power, the surrender of Life itself. It is the supreme consummation of sacrifice, than which none can be higher or greater.

To lay down life for friends, that is glorious selfless, inspiring! But to re-enact the tragedy of Calvary for generations yet unborn, that is the last consummate sacrifice of the Militant!

The end game had arrived. Davison's spirits were not down-cast, however. She was said to have joined the May Day celebrations in Hyde Park in 1913, at which the crowds boomed out 'La Marseillaise', 'The Red Flag' and other socialist anthems. She told *The Times*: 'I felt a revolutionary of the revolutionaries and ready and proud to take part in any great demonstration for the liberties of the people ... We felt ourselves to be the heirs of all the ages and sires of the great, great future.'[47]

On 7 May the news broke that a second attempt in Par-liament to introduce women's suffrage via a private member's bill had failed. Willoughby Dickinson, a Liberal MP, had made a second bid in the Commons six years after his first attempt. Its defeat by forty-five votes came as little surprise to the weary suffragettes, but impressed again the feeling held by many that Parliament was intractably opposed to their cause.[48]

On the last day of May, Davison attended a lecture at the Bishopsgate Institute in east London, hosted by the Workers' Educational Association. With her was Miss Clarke, a friend whom she had met when they had both worked as stewards at the Great Central Railway's Marylebone Station during the protest in Hyde Park in 1908. The association's official newspaper, *The Highway*, reported after Davison's death that throughout that day 'she was urging the claims of the As-sociation in the whole-hearted way so characteristic of her'. The eulogy continued: 'Hers was a sunny, cheerful nature and in the W.E.A. it had full play. The stress of her life lay outside our limits, but with us she was happy as amongst friends. We are glad of it, and shall never forget her joyous presence.'

After the lecture, the two friends took tea in Holborn and chatted for two hours. Tellingly, Miss Clarke said afterwards: 'Emily was in an expansive mood, disposed to talk, to linger, showing more affection than it was her fashion to display.' She was only four days away from the Derby, and almost exactly a year on from her previous attempt at making a grand gesture in hurling herself down Holloway's iron staircase.

Three days before she went to the Derby she received another final note of rejection from a prospective employer. Robert Field of the *Daily Citizen* wrote her an ill-tempered missive, in which he expressed frustration that she had hassled him about a submission. 'If you had as many preoccupations as I have, you would better understand why I have been such a dilatory letter-writer,' he said. Turning to the poem she had submitted, he added: 'I have worried over it a great deal trying to decide what the author intended. The idea is quite good but the workmanship leaves something to be desired.' The terse appraisal of her verse was, at least, tempered with the offer of a cup of tea and a chat.[49]

On Tuesday 3 June, Davison attended the opening day of the suffragettes' summer fête, entitled 'All in a Garden Fair', at the Empress Rooms, Kensington. Upon arrival she steered Mary Leigh to go and gaze with her at the statue of Joan of Arc, the patron saint of the WSPU and Davison's personal heroine (Joan of Arc had been beatified in 1909 and would go on to be declared a saint in 1920), which resided in the gardens. The pair stood side by side and read the inscription: 'Fight on and God will give the victory'. A month previously the iconic militant, pictured in full armour on horseback, had graced the front page of *The Suffragette*. Christabel Pankhurst had written in the newspaper:

> Joan of Arc lives on as the glory and inspiration of France. To British women also she has left a great inheritance ... of simplicity, purity, courage, and militancy ... She belongs to the womanhood of the whole world, and the women of our country are one with the men and women of France in adoring her memory.[50]

Davison spent the day at the fair, enjoying the games on offer and browsing stalls selling books printed by the Women's Press[xxi] and photographs of the most famous suffragettes. The aim was to raise money for the activists' war fund.

At the event Davison saw Kitty Marion, an actress who had gained distinction in the WSPU for setting fire to her cell while imprisoned for militant action in 1909. She gave Marion that day a 'tiny green chamois purse containing a sovereign for munitions I might need', the actress later recalled.

Davison meanwhile told Leigh that she would come to the fair every day 'except tomorrow', adding: 'I'm going to the Derby tomorrow'. Leigh asked her what plans she had

---

xxi   The WSPU set up the Women's Press in 1908 to publish their newspaper. In 1910 the Union opened a shop by the same name at Clement's Inn, London, to help raise revenue and publicise their cause.

for the following day that were so important they would keep her away from the suffragettes' summer celebration. Teasingly vague, Davison replied: 'Look in the evening paper and you will see something.'[51]

CHAPTER 10

AN INTRUDER AT THE DERBY
4–8 JUNE 1913

Wednesday 4 June 1913 was Derby Day and the last sentient day of Davison's life. She awoke early in London at the house of her friend Alice Green on Clapham Road, Lambeth, where she had been lodging.[52] She went to the WSPU headquarters and asked for two suffragette Union flags, each measuring 1.4 metres by 0.7 metres, in the familiar colours of purple, green and white. When asked what purpose she intended for the flags, a contemporary said that Davison mysteriously replied simply: 'Ah!' Mary Leigh accepted her friend's reticence and said, 'Perhaps I'd better not ask.' Davison agreed: 'Don't ask me.' The WSPU leadership later stressed that any action she took that day was without their knowledge or approval.

Davison left the headquarters and went directly to Victoria railway station, where she bought a return ticket and caught the train to Epsom Downs. She was part of the vast throng of Londoners headed to the racecourse that day, which was perhaps the great high day and holiday of the era. It was a day out on the downs, with no admission charge, and alongside the racing featured funfairs, performers and trinket- and food-sellers. The revellers arrived by train, bus, carriage and cart for an afternoon of jollity; King George V and his wife Queen Mary also took up place in the royal box accompanied by numerous courtiers. Edwardian ladies and gentlemen in their finest couture were present alongside factory workers. It was a rare occasion in which Britons from all classes were represented, though they remained segregated in different areas.

Joining the crowd of 60,000 or more racegoers, Davison did not stand out. She was dressed plainly and did nothing in the early part of the day to draw attention to herself. She bought a Dorling's List of Epsom Races, scoured the form of the horses and marked down which she fancied as winners. Right up until the great race of the day, Davison followed almost every other event. The race card found on her person after she was carried unconscious from the course bore witness to a bet she had placed just thirty minutes beforehand. It was not obviously the behaviour of someone who intended to risk their life within the hour.

Just before 3 p.m., the horses paraded near the grandstand. Anmer, the King's horse, led the procession. He was to be ridden by the royal jockey Herbert Jones, who had already won two Derbies for the King: riding Diamond Jubilee in

1900 and again on Minoru in 1909. Also in the field were a little-fancied horse called Aboyeur as well as the hot favourite, Craganour. The latter horse was the equine celebrity of the year, and was under round-the-clock guard after threats had been received from suffragettes, or those posing as them, to prevent the horse from running. The security proved effective, however, and Craganour came to Epsom leading the betting as the 6/4 favourite.

As the horses made their way up the hill to the start, the crowds were jostling; pushing and shoving to get a clear view of the race. Some took the high ground, some clambered onto the top decks of the omnibuses that had brought them there, but most tried to carve out a place by the stout white rails that studded the course. Thousands of people lined up along the barriers of the racecourse. With such a potentially raucous rabble, a sturdy police presence was established along the track, numbering more than fifty officers. Sergeant Frank Bunn, an on-duty policeman, moved to where the scrum was densest. As the crowds grew he would become pressed up against them near Davison. She stood by the rail on the commoners' side of the racecourse, far from the fashionable grandstand and stationed at the point where the sweeping downhill curve of Tattenham Corner meets the straight.

As the crowds took to their places to watch the great race, the camera crews, taking full advantage of the sensational new technology that had led to the invention of newsreels, also took up position. Pathé Gazette, Topical Budget and Gaumont Graphic were the three companies present and it is, in part, their dramatic footage of what ensued during the race that has shocked audiences for the past century – and assured Davison's fame.

Fellow suffragette Mary Richardson also said she had been at Epsom that day, determined, in a modest way, to represent the cause. She later wrote: 'Just as the first race began I summoned up all my courage and took out a copy of *The Suffragette* from my bag and waved it in the air. I had judged correctly: except for the scornful glances cast in my direction I was not molested.' A little while before the great race she saw Davison. She recalled:

It was not until the end of the third race that I saw Emily Davison. We have met several times and from the talks we had I had formed the opinion that she was a very serious-minded person. That was why I felt so surprised to see her. She was not the sort of woman to spend an afternoon at the races. I smiled to her; and from the distance she seemed to be smiling faintly back at me. She stood alone there, close to the white-painted rails where the course bends round at Tattenham Corner; she looked absorbed and yet far away from everybody else and seemed to have no interest in what was going on round her.

The integrity of Richardson's account is not infallible. Her presence at a number of key events has proven difficult for historians to corroborate, while her desire to become a novelist has led to conjecture that she 'may have encouraged her pen to run away with itself'.[53] The excitable Canadian-born suffragette, who used the nom de guerre 'Polly Dick', was keen to be at the centre of events. It is odd indeed, however, that if she had not been privy to Davison's plans on the racecourse that she should have found herself by chance standing so close in a crowd of thousands. Other reports placed her there, though historians later speculated that if a suffragette was present, it was likely Mary Leigh. In one report that named Richardson, she was described as the WSPU pipe major, a role that in fact belonged to Leigh.[54]

The dramatist St John Ervine, who was then working as a journalist, was another eyewitness. He remembered Davison as less calm, recalling 'a rather agitated woman', who was 'very pale and thin' and 'quite clearly in a state of mental agitation'.

As the great race began, Davison steadied herself for her planned manoeuvre. Richardson, in her questionable testimony, later purported to have witnessed Davison's intrusion on the course. She wrote:

I was unable to keep my eyes off her as I stood holding *The Suffragette* up in my clenched hand. A minute before the race started she raised a paper of her own or some kind of card before her eyes. I was watching her hand. It did not shake. Even when I heard the pounding of the horses' hooves moving closer I saw she was still smiling.

She went on:

I felt a sudden premonition about her and found my heart was beating excitedly. I shall always remember how beautifully calm her face was. But at that very moment – as I was told afterwards by her closest friend – she knew she was about to give her life for the cause.

Standing beside Davison, St John Ervine recalled looking up the course and seeing the horses galloping in their direction 'like express trains'. By the time the horses reached Tattenham Corner, the field had split into two tightly grouped packs. Aboyeur was leading the field of fifteen horses. Nine horses in the first group sped past, and then there was a gap. Anmer, the King's horse, was in the second group, which came careering around the corner in a 30-mile-per-hour stampede. The *New York Times* reported: 'Coming round Tattenham Corner, the rear of the race was brought up by Agadir, Anmer, and Bachelor's Wedding in the order named. People were hanging dangerously over the rails at the point where the jockeys hug the turn, and a policeman was warning them to keep back.'

Davison, tall and slender, dipped nimbly under the railings and rushed out briskly onto the track. She did not run or fling herself, but demonstrated nerve and a chilling calmness. She dodged out of the way of the other oncoming galloping horses such as Agadir as if she was aiming only for the King's mount. Contemporary newsreel appears to show that Anmer alone was her target.

As Anmer came towards her, free from other horses both ahead and behind, she leapt upon his bridle and swung round in front of the horse. The horse swerved, then fell and the jockey Herbert Jones was hurled off. He crashed to the ground with one foot trapped in the stirrup and was dragged several yards before managing to roll free. Davison was thrown about thirty feet backwards along the course in the direction of the horse's travel by the force of the impact. The horse lost its footing and fell upon her. Her short-brimmed hat, pinned with a carnation, tumbled to the ground, wheeling along the turf behind her.

An eyewitness account from a *Manchester Guardian* report stated:

The horse fell on the woman and kicked out furiously, and it was sickening to see his hooves strike her repeatedly. It all happened in a flash before we had time to realise it was over. The horse struggled to its feet – I don't think it was hurt – but the jockey and the woman lay on the ground. It was a terrible thing.

Another man present said:

We were all intent on the finish of the race, and were straining forward to see which of the leaders had won. Just at that moment there was a scream, and I saw a woman leaping forward and making a grab at the bridle of Anmer, the King's horse … The woman was lying on the ground, and when the crowd rushed on to the course the police surrounded her. She was removed on a stretcher.

St John Ervine said both the jockey and Davison

> were bleeding profusely, but the crowd which swarmed
> about them was immediately too much for me to see
> any more. I feel sure that Ms Davison meant to stop the
> horses, and that she did not go on to the course in the
> belief that the race was over, for, as I say, only a few of the
> horses had gone by when I first saw her leave the railings,
> and others had not passed when she was knocked down …
> The affair distressed the crowd very much.[55]

Richardson claimed to have watched bystanders invade the
course, though she may well have relied on newsreel footage
in her account of what happened next. She wrote:

> It was all over so quickly. Emily was under the hooves for
> some distance across the grass. The horse stumbled side-
> ways and its jockey was thrown from its back. She lay very
> still. There was an awful silence that seemed to go on for
> minutes; then, suddenly, angry shouts and cries arose and
> people swarmed out on to the racecourse. I was rooted to
> the earth with horror until a man snatched the paper I was
> still holding in my hand and beat it across my face.

The Times concluded afterwards that the horses had come
so quickly that Davison could not have possibly known she
was seizing the reins to the King's horse. The paper said:
'The general impression of those who saw the incident at

close quarters seemed to be that the woman had seized hold of the first horse she could reach – which happened to be the King's. That the horse was the King's was doubtless an accident.' Even the coroner at her inquest, Gilbert White, concluded she could not have attacked Anmer specifically.

This opinion is not shared by all the experts who have studied the film of the incident. One commentator surmised in the *Racing Post*:[xxii] 'The newsreel confirms that Davison deliberately avoided Agadir and the next two horses, after which there was another gap to Anmer, and two stragglers. It is impossible to be certain that she knew the horse's identity but that was the horse Davison deliberately stood in front of.' The Pathé footage shows Emily walking – almost wafting – between several other horses before seeming to stand fractionally to the side of Anmer's path before grabbing at, or being hit by, the horse – it is difficult to make a conclusive judgment. She may have had time to see the distinctive purple, scarlet and gold of the royal jockey's silks.

Newsreel footage exists from various angles and conclusions can be drawn from a comparison of the British Pathé[56] and Gaumont[57] film. Davison's arms were raised as she approached the horse, whether to shield the sun from her eyes, or to protect her head and face, is unclear. It is possible she had them up in readiness to clutch on to Anmer's bridle. In any case, she was not clutching either of the two flags she had collected earlier in the morning.

---

xxii   David Ashforth, 2006.

Herbert Jones, then twenty-eight years old, suffered concussion and was knocked unconscious for two hours. He was tended to by a racegoer who happened to be a doctor and was later removed to the ambulance room at the course, where he was examined further. The official police report stated he suffered from 'abrasion on left of face, abrasion over left eye and shoulder, contusion of left elbow and shock'. Eventually he regained consciousness and was left in the charge of the doctors. Confused and in shock after the incident, he refused to go to hospital. A friend with whom the jockey lived took him to a nearby hotel later that night to recover. His horse Anmer was, in the event, fine, even though he had been pitched over onto his head. Rider-less, he wandered off and was eventually stopped on the course. He was handed over to a Newmarket trainer. The horse suffered cuts on its face and body, and damaged one of its fore-hooves.

After the collision between Davison and Anmer, there were cries of panic and horror from the crowd. Some of the racegoers began to invade the turf, some of them to help the jockey and the woman. At that stage, no one had the faintest idea that Davison was a suffragette; the flags she had taken were tacked on the inside of her coat. She was, many presumed, a confused and possibly drunk woman who had wandered onto the course during the premier race of the year.

A doctor from Banstead, Surrey, called Jasper Vale-Lane rushed to Davison's side and attended to her. Later that evening he would write: 'I was the first to render medical assistance to the woman. I took charge of the case. I found her suffering from concussion of the brain and heart failure and her life ebbing fast.' A nurse who happened to be standing nearby, named in the police report as Mrs Warburg from Paddington, London, also helped. Davison was judged by the doctor to be in a critical condition. Whisky was administered to her limp lips and hot tea applied to her wrist to revive her pulse, the doctor wrote.

She was scooped up and carried to a motorcar in which she was driven, with Mrs Warburg alongside her, to Epsom Cottage Hospital. She was examined by the house surgeon, Dr Peacock, who confirmed that she was suffering from severe concussion. She remained unconscious and in a critical condition.

Although some racegoers did not learn of the tragedy until they read the papers the next day, word of the incident swiftly reached the royal box. The King was horrified to learn of the injuries to his jockey. Herbert Jones had long ridden for the royal family and his winning three of the five English classic races in 1900 on the Prince of Wales's horse, Diamond Jubilee, had earned him the nickname 'Diamond' Jones. King George left the box and went down to the Jockey Club terraces to inquire as to the condition of his jockey. Assured that the jockey was not mortally wounded, he asked to be personally updated on any developments with Herbert's health by the attendant police chief, Superintendent McCarthy. The King, showing where his sympathies lay, later wrote in his diary that the Derby had been a 'most disappointing day', noting down ruefully that 'poor Herbert Jones and Anmer had been sent flying'.

Queen Mary's first thought was also for 'poor Jones'; she referred to Davison, meanwhile, as 'the horrid woman'. In a telegram she wished Jones a swift recovery after his 'sad accident caused through the abominable conduct of a brutal lunatic woman'. Dr Vale-Lane later reported to the King and Queen that Davison had been seriously injured, though no enquiry was made by the pair thereafter as to her condition. They did keep abreast of the recovery of the jockey and were glad to learn from the doctor that he had enjoyed a lucky escape.

Given Davison's actions, the horse race itself has unsurprisingly become one of history's afterthoughts. It was, however, one of the most controversial races of the time in its own right, due to its disputed result. The leading group of horses had included Aboyeur, the 100/1 shot who had been at the front from the start, Craganour, the favourite, plus Louvois, Shogun and Day Comet. They were tightly bunched, with Aboyeur and Craganour just ahead. In the final furlongs, the two horses clashed. Most reports have it that Aboyeur, ridden by Edwin Piper, was initially in the wrong, but Craganour, ridden by American jockey Johnny Reiff, certainly retaliated. As they all crossed the line, Craganour was in front, closely followed by Aboyeur, and the favourite's number was duly posted in the winner's slot. The stewards judging the race objected to the winner, however, a distinctly unusual turn of events. There was a lengthy delay while they deliberated, before declaring Aboyeur, known previously as an aggressive horse, the winner, with Craganour placed second and

Louvois third, although photographic evidence showed that Day Comet had crossed the line ahead of Louvois.

The race was a scandal and there may have been a dark motive behind the disputed finish. Craganour was owned by Charles Bower Ismay. He was the younger brother of J. Bruce Ismay, managing director of the White Star Line, the owners of the RMS *Titanic*, which had sunk just fourteen months before with the loss of more than 1,500 lives. J. Bruce Ismay had been on board, but had survived, getting away in one of the last lifeboats. Widely condemned as a despicable coward he was, by 1913, one of the most reviled men in Britain. Adding to the brew of ill-feeling, Epsom steward Eustace Loder had apparently long-harboured a grudge against Craganour's stable owner for having an affair with his sister-in-law. Not merely for the bumping and biting by the horses in the home straight was this 1913 race known thereafter as 'The Dirty Derby'.

Davison's actions could have won the battle for the overarching narrative of the Derby among racing enthusiasts, however. Her actions – whatever her motives – endangered the lives of more than just one jockey and horse. Several historians have considered the counterfactual scenario in which Davison survived, but Jones the jockey was killed. It was a far from improbable outcome and, if it had occurred, would have cast Davison in a far less celebrated light in future decades.

Given the speed of the horses and the chaotic nature of them hurtling in a group down off Tattenham Corner, the outcome was outside of Davison's control. Thus it was that her actions prompted the next day's headlines 'Suffragist's mad act' and 'Sensational Derby'. Many papers concentrated their attention on the surprise result and controversy of the horse race itself, however: the 100/1 outsider winning after the favourite, Craganour, was disqualified in a controversial finish. The *Daily Mirror* wrote of the indignation of all those who had witnessed Davison's actions and concentrated on the resentment felt towards the suffragettes after the incident. 'But for her obviously serious injuries, she would have undoubtedly fared badly at the hands of the crowd', who displayed an 'evident desire to lynch her', the paper reported.

All the newspapers carried dramatic accounts of the Derby and many featured editorials damning her behaviour. Her high profile by 1913 was attested in the press reports that followed. The day after her death *The Times* called her 'one of the most prominent of the militant women suffragists'.

In line with much popular sentiment and, firmly on the side of the establishment, many papers eschewed restraint in their treatment of the radical activist. The *Daily Express* printed a particularly scathing obituary under the headline 'Blighted by Militancy … Ruined career'. The paper described a

story of a brilliant career, marred with an ignominious death as its conclusion … The pathetic loneliness to which Miss Davison's career of militancy had brought her was illustrated by the evidence of a police sergeant named Frank Bunn. Describing his efforts to render assistance to the unconscious woman as she lay on the course after the accident, he said: 'I called out among the crowd, "Does anyone know this woman?" But there was no reply.'

The following day's *Northern Echo* described the incident as 'a desperate assault, a mad scheme and the recklessness of the fanatic'. Davison's behaviour was variously described as 'mad', 'demented', 'wicked' and 'folly'. The *Manchester Guardian* at least admitted to its connection with her, stating that 'Emily Wilding Davison was a frequent contributor to *Guardian* correspondence columns.'

On the racecourse, however, the police and hospital authorities were dealing with the aftermath of a very serious incident. Sergeant Frank Bunn, the policeman on duty near Davison, filed an official report at his station in Epsom. It read:

I beg to report that at 3.10pm 4th inst. I was on duty at Tattenham Corner near the tan path whilst the race for the Derby Cup was being run. Several horses passed by when a woman, supposed Emily Davison, ran out from under the fence and held her hands up in front of HM King's horse, whereby she was knocked down and rendered unconscious.

Davison had fallen into a deep coma by the time she had reached Epsom Cottage Hospital. There it was discovered that she had a fractured skull and severe internal injuries. A police guard was called to protect the near-lifeless suffragette from an angry crowd, while Dr Peacock was appointed to take charge of her.

Eleanor Penn Gaskell, who rushed to her friend's bedside, wrote in a letter to another friend, a Miss Dixon, that their comrade had improved at first.

Our heroine is now partly conscious, that is to say she shows recognition when addressed by name and can take food but makes no attempt to speak. It is thought she may remain much in this state for about a fortnight but in any case will not be able to be moved for a fortnight. The injury is to the head, the extent will not be ascertained for a fortnight – no bones broken. Her head struck the horse – she suffers no pain. She makes slight favourable progress and I think that is all there is to be said. We must wait patiently … they are most kind at the little hospital and she lacks for nothing … What splendid courage. What a wonderful message she has sent through the length and breadth of the land. I am sure the sacrifice will not be in vain. I wish I could give you more definite and better news but it is early days yet and the injury of course was very serious.[58]

Davison's great friend Charles Mansell Moullin, a doctor who had helped her with her health following arduous prison stints and the husband of her friend Edith, arrived to care for her as life ebbed out of her battered body. He was a Harley Street surgeon and a fellow of the Royal College of

Surgeons. Additionally, as a member of the Men's League for Women's Suffrage (MLWS) and a respected medical practitioner, he had also protested against forcible feeding from a medical point of view for some years.

On Friday 6 June, he operated on Davison's skull, in a bid to relieve pressure on her brain. At first the operation seemed to have been a success and provided the intended relief, but she never fully regained consciousness.

His report on Davison's health was printed in *The Suffragette* on 13 June 1913. It read in part:

> The shock of the injuries she had sustained was so severe that for some time it was not thought that she would rally at all. On Thursday afternoon her pulse was a little better, but it was evident that there was bleeding going on inside the skull from a fracture across the base, and from the injured brain. On Friday an operation was performed which gave great temporary relief, but the injured portion of the brain never recovered, and the heart and the breathing gradually failed. Miss Davison was completely unconscious, never opening her eyes or speaking from the moment the horse struck her until the end. Dr Thornley and Dr Peacock showed her every possible attention, and the matron and staff were kindness itself.

Several of Davison's closest suffragette companions joined her relatives, and Penn Gaskell, at her bedside as soon as they heard the news. Among them were Mary Leigh and Rose

Lamartine Yates, who described Davison as 'my comrade, and my old college friend' (the pair having attended Holloway together). Lamartine Yates had the task of telephoning Davison's mother Margaret to inform her of events. Margaret later wrote to her about her 'dear daughter's sacrifice' and thanked the suffragette for persuading her husband Thomas to arrange for Davison's essay, 'The Price of Liberty', to be printed after her death. In a letter to Margaret she expressed her thanks to Thomas 'for his letter and the *Daily Sketch* 28 May containing that beautiful message from dear Emily … I feel most grateful to your husband for all he has done for me and send him my sincere thanks'.

The Times reported on 9 June:

A number of lady friends called at the Epsom Cottage Hospital on Saturday afternoon to inquire as to the condition of Miss Davison. Two visitors draped the screen round the bed with the W.S.P.U. colours and tied the W.S.P.U. badge to the head of the bed. A sister of Miss Davison and a lady friend of her mother stayed at the hospital for many hours, and on Saturday night Captain Davison, a brother of the patient, arrived.

As they did so, the Director of Public Prosecutions decided that, should Davison recover, 'it will be possible to charge her with doing an act calculated to cause grievous bodily harm'.

Hate mail also arrived for the comatose suffragette. One bilious missive, signed 'an Englishman', stated:

I am glad to hear that you are in hospital. I hope you suffer torture until you die. You idiot. I consider you are a person un-worthy of existence in this world, considering what you have done. I should like the opportunity of starving and beating you to a pulp. Why don't your people find an asylum for you?[59]

A second letter, signed 'A. Roused', said:

I as sincerely wish for your recovery as I regret that it is pos-sible. When you are fully conscious it may be that the crazy fanaticism which drove you to break the laws of God and Man will have left your poor brain clearer. And in that case surely you will thank Him for sparing you the sin of murder! Of course, I cannot hope to touch the heart of a confirmed goal bird...[60]

While Davison lay unconscious, a letter remained unopened by her bed. Scrawled on the envelope were the words: 'Please give this to Emily'. It was from her mother, written while there was still hope of her recovery. 'I cannot believe that you could have done such a dreadful act,' she wrote. 'Even for the Cause which I know you have given up your whole heart and soul to, and it has done so little in return for you.

'Now I can only hope and pray that God will mercifully restore you to life and health and that there may be a better and brighter future for you.' There was no future, save as a martyr for her cause. At 4.50 p.m. on Sunday 8 June, four days after her collision with Herbert Jones and Anmer, Emily

Wilding Davison died. None of her family or friends were with her as she slipped away.

Two weeks later, there was an odd copycat sequel to the event. It came during the running of the Gold Cup at Ascot, also a premier race, when a young man waving a suffragette flag and brandishing a revolver ran onto the course. He stood in the way of the leading horse – Tracery, the second-favourite – and called on the jockey to stop. There was no chance of that happening, and in the resultant collision the intruder was seriously injured, though the horse was unharmed and the jockey only shaken. The copycat was taken to a nearby hospital, operated upon, and eventually recovered.

His name was Harold Hewitt and he was the forty-year-old scion of a respectable and wealthy family. Educated at Harrow and Trinity College, Cambridge, he had apparently been leading a nomadic existence in South Africa and elsewhere. His late father owned Hope End, a large estate in Herefordshire, where the poet Elizabeth Barrett Browning had once lived. He was thought to have been at Emily Davison's funeral and inspired by her death, but the notebook found on his person was reported to be full of disjointed statements, the revolver he carried had been loaded and he had been carrying cash to the tune of £200 (about £3,000 today) at the time of his accident. Friends had said he had recently spoken of suicide.

As soon as Hewitt recovered from his injuries he was placed in an asylum. From here he escaped, however, and made his way to Canada, where he farmed for several years.

Then, in January 1921, out of the blue, he returned to England and gave himself up to face a charge of having caused bodily harm to the jockey, Albert 'Snowy' Whalley. A week later he was found guilty and sentenced to a mere two days in prison. Nothing more is known of the curious imitator of Emily Wilding Davison.

CHAPTER 11

SUICIDE, MISADVENTURE OR MARTYRDOM? 10–13 JUNE 1913

D avison's inquest was scheduled for 10 June at Epsom Court House, a cramped little red-brick police court just up from the crossroads in the centre of town. Police Sergeant Frank Bunn, who had been on duty at the racecourse on 4 June, offered an eyewitness account of her death. The coroner, Gilbert H. White, asked him as to his opinion of whether Davison had picked out Anmer, the King's horse, specifically. 'I do not think it would be possible the way they were bunched together,' the sergeant replied. He confirmed his belief that the action was deliberate, however, and the coroner ruled that Davison had not marked the King's horse as her target, but had merely intended to disturb the race.

Police Constable Eady, who had been standing just forty yards from the straight of the racecourse, also testified. He stated that he had seen Davison's head duck out from under the bar upon which she had been leaning just as the horses were passing. One horse swerved past her, while another shortly afterwards struck her as she stood in the middle of the course – with its front feet, he said.

The injured jockey, Herbert Jones, was not well enough to testify to the court. Margaret, Davison's mother, could not bear the thought of attending the proceedings, so Rose and Thomas Lamartine Yates went in her place. Davison's half-brother, Captain Henry Jocelyn Davison, was also present and was called upon to give evidence. He is said to have described his sister as a graduate of London University who had taken classical honours at Oxford, adding: 'She was a person of considerable gifts as a speaker and writer.'[61]

The foreman of the jury asked him: 'Did you know anything that would lead you to think that she was abnormal mentally?' He replied firmly: 'Nothing.' When questioned by Thomas Lamartine Yates, he insisted his sister was of very strong reasoning faculties and passionately devoted to the women's movement. He went on to say that the only explanation he could conjure for her actions at the Derby was that she had intended to draw attention to the suffrage movement. Curiously, however, he was sure that it was an accident. He argued that while she realised the danger and accepted it, she nonetheless would have believed that she would be saved from it. It is notable that he stressed her intelligence and age – she was, after all, a middle-aged woman, and not the whimsical girl she is sometimes portrayed as in the prolific retelling of her story.

Lamartine Yates tried to make a political point, asking the witness whether he thought his sister's behaviour was a bid to call public attention specifically to the fact that the government had not done justice to women, but the coroner intervened and made clear he would allow no questioning along these lines. After hearing evidence of her being taken to Epsom Cottage Hospital, and the attention she received there before her death, the coroner concluded, according to *The Times* of 11 June:

> It was evident that Miss Davison did not make specially for the King's horse, but her intention was merely to disturb or upset the race. If they [the jury] found that this was her intention they would probably be of the opinion that it was a death by misadventure. Her object was not, he thought, to take her own life.

After an absence of one hour and twenty-five minutes, the jury returned with their verdict: 'That Miss Emily Wilding Davison died of fracture of the base of the skull, caused by being accidentally knocked down by a horse through wilfully rushing on to the racecourse on Epsom Downs during the progress of the race for the Derby; death was due to misadventure.' As far as the official record went, she died an accidental martyr – not, in all likelihood, the verdict she would have wished for herself.

The coroner endorsed the verdict of death by misadventure, and Davison's death certificate duly stated that she died from a fracture at the base of the skull after having deliberately intruded on the racecourse at Epsom Downs. Her family would likely have been relieved that her death had not been judged a suicide, a verdict that would have barred her from being buried on consecrated ground alongside other family members in the graveyard of St Mary's in Morpeth. Her comrades in the movement, meanwhile, may have baulked at the 'misadventure' verdict, which jarred with the narrative of her making an intentional sacrifice in the name of women's suffrage.

The coroner said: 'It is exceedingly sad – so it seems to me – that an educated lady should sacrifice her life in such a way.' The one bureaucratic task remaining was the processing of her will. Some time later, probate was granted to her mother, to whom she left her entire worldly wealth: £186 1s 7d (about £2,800 today).

Misadventure may have been the official verdict on her death, but it was by no means the final one. Ever since 4 June 1913, Davison's intention that day has been picked and fought over.

Her mother Margaret had said in her final letter to her daughter, which went unread: 'I know that you would not willfully [sic] give me any unhappiness.' She went on, fleshing out her view of her child's actions on Derby Day: 'It must have been some sudden impulse and excitement.'[62]

Another theory that has gained currency posited that Davison's actions at the Derby had not been of her own device. Tantalisingly, references abound to a telegram sent to her a week before Derby Day, instructing her to go to Epsom. This theory relies on accounts of local friends in Longhorsley that held Davison to have been subdued and patently distracted after receiving the alleged telegram at home in the north-east.[63] Unfortunately if it did exist, its sender and its contents remain a mystery. Some commentators have surmised, however, that if there was such a message, then its ultimate source was likely Christabel Pankhurst, who by this time was based in Paris in order to avoid arrest. Others have insisted the telegram derived from a group of local suffragettes in the north-east, pointing to claims that some time before Derby Day straws had been drawn by a gathering of local female activists to choose a demonstrator to cause a scene at Epsom.[64] However, while Davison had always shown herself wiling to undertake risky missions, she had rarely been one to take orders or cleave to the plans of a group. Strong-minded and independent, she had always tended to be the author of her own actions.

The thesis that can be most safely eliminated immediately is that which contended Davison had merely tried to cross the racecourse from one side to another. Some spectators told the papers their impression had been that the woman had intended to get to a friend on the opposite side and fainted when she saw the horses galloping towards her. The suggestion, outlandish in nature, is refuted by the newsreel footage.

Clearly Davison had intended to confront a horse in the main race of the day and to cause a stir – but how and to what end remain disputed questions. The first conundrum surrounding her actions involved the train ticket she bought to Epsom Downs at Victoria railway station – crucially, a return fare. The purchase of a two-way ticket has been claimed by some historians as conclusive proof she intended to return to the capital at the end of the day and therefore did not envisage sustaining injury – or even arrest. It seems possible, however, that it was an oversight, a purchase made under pressure amid jostling crowds, money unthinkingly exchanged with the clerk – a scenario compatible with her travelling to the Downs with a plan in mind to intrude on the Derby. It is equally as possible that she planned to make the tragic gesture, but calculated that if the circumstances evaded her, she may as well have a ticket home at the ready. A third theory that allows for the scenario that her intention before travelling had been to make a dangerous protest is that the rail authorities had simply produced returns to make it easier to wave the unusually large crowds onto the trains, expecting the vast majority to return that evening.

The return ticket to London was not the only item Davison had with her as she walked on to the racecourse. According to the police report, the personal effects found in her pockets and on her person were: the two WSPU flags; stamps; her helper's pass for the four-day suffragette Summer Festival at the Empress Rooms, Kensington; a notebook; a race card; and a handkerchief on which was embroidered her name.[xxiii]

---

xxiii   The personal effects found on Davison were given, after her death, to her
friend, Rose Lamartine Yates.

In addition, in her purse was a newspaper cutting from *The Times* about the death of the Reverend Forbes Jackson, who was survived by a widow and six children. The newspaper clearly asserted that Davison was the cause of his demise, though it did not name her.[65]

The WSPU flags attest to a plan to make a suffragette protest of some sort. The fact that she had them pinned inside her coat is a strong indication that, if seriously injured, they would bear silent witness to the cause she was representing. The idea that she was planning to stop the King's horse, galloping at thirty miles per hour, produce a flag and pin it to the horse's saddle in a publicity stunt seems highly fanciful, especially given where the flags were found on her person. Police Inspector G. Whitebread reported:

> The suffragette colours were not tied round the woman's waist but were pinned to the inside of her jacket, apparently to act as a pad for her back. The flags were completely hidden in the back of her jacket. The flags were not seen until the woman's jacket was removed at the Cottage Hospital. No-one in the vicinity had any idea that the woman was a militant suffragette until the flags were found.

Furthermore, during an age in which the use of horses as a means of transportation and an instrument in leisure activities was far greater than in modern times, it seems improbable that Davison would have been so naïve as to think she could hope to pin anything to a galloping horse, with or without sustaining severe injury.

Some historians have argued that she did not intend to kill herself, but merely bring down the King's horse and stop the race. Sylvia Pankhurst wrote in her 1931 book, *The Suffragette Movement*:

> With a fellow-militant in whose flat she lived, she had concerted a Derby protest without tragedy – a mere waving of the purple-white-and-green at Tattenham Corner, which, by its suddenness, it was hoped would stop the race. Whether from the first her purpose was more serious, or whether a final impulse altered her resolve, I know not. Her friend declares she would not thus have died without writing a farewell message to her mother. Yet she had sewed the W.S.P.U. colours inside her coat as though to ensure that no mistake could be made as to her motive when her dead body should be examined. So she set forth alone, the hope of a great achievement surging through her mind. With sure resolve she ran out onto the course and deliberately flung herself upon the King's horse, Anmer, that her deed might be the more pointed.

Herbert Jones, who was riding Anmer in the Derby, was always adamant that to his mind Davison had not intended to collide with him and the horse. He believed that she had planned merely to intrude onto the course, possibly brandish a suffragette flag in front of the vast throng, and no doubt be arrested. He asserted that where she had been standing in the crowd, at the end of the sharpish bend, meant that she could not see, until she dipped under the rail, if the course was clear or not. He was always inclined to think she had assumed, when the leading group of runners had passed, that the coast was clear. No one could doubt Jones's sincerity – the trainer he rode for, Richard Marsh, said of him: 'A straighter or more honest jockey never got on a horse' – but he nonetheless had a motive to convince himself it was a terrible accident.

Emmeline Pankhurst, for her own part, concluded that Davison had sacrificed her life for the cause. 'Emily Davison clung to her conviction that one great tragedy, the deliberate throwing into the breach of human life, would put an end to the intolerable torture of women,' she said. 'And so she threw herself at the King's horse in full view of the King and Queen and a great multitude of their Majesties' subjects.' But then the leader of the WSPU had her own reasons for claiming Davison as a martyr to the cause.

Lady Constance Lytton, Davison's former comrade-in-arms, also thought her friend's purpose at the Derby had been to make the ultimate sacrifice in the name of women's suffrage. As one of Davison's closest allies, she can perhaps be trusted to make a better guess at intent than most. She wrote a year after the incident:

In 1913 she [Emily Davison] met her death with the most heroic courage at the Derby race. It was her opportunity of proclaiming to the whole world, perhaps heedless till then, that women claim citizenship and human rights. She stood in front of the race and was knocked down by the King's horse Anmer, rendered unconscious, and died the following Sunday, June 8. Millions of people, not only in our own but other countries, knew, from this act, that there are women who care so passionately for the vote and all it means that they are willing to die for it.

Another close friend, Eleanor Penn Gaskell, wrote: 'Knowing Emily Davison as I did, I can clearly read the meaning of this supreme sacrifice.' Rose Lamartine Yates declared: 'She had felt the call, she knew that suffering and outraged womanhood looked to her.'

Mary Richardson, the suffragette who was purportedly at Epsom that day, came up with a strange account that seemed to take full advantage of hindsight. She wrote later: 'It is impossible to explain feelings like that; one can only accept them and wonder. The evening before the Derby Emily had told a few friends, quite calmly, that she would be the only casualty. No one else would be injured, not even the jockey.' Nobody identified themselves in the immediate aftermath or in later decades as being a confidante to Davison ahead of Derby Day, however. Perhaps Richardson's claims were intended merely as a post-hoc attempt to rebut the argument that Davison's actions were reckless and could have ended in more deaths than only hers. The idea that anyone, even if they had rehearsed time and again, could possibly have ensured that they, the intruder, were the only casualty from such an action is fanciful. Bemusingly, there have even been some writers who claim there were reports that Emily and other suffragists had been seen in Northumberland over the preceding weeks practising grabbing the reins of running horses. It seems far-fetched, and no witness has ever come forward.

So did Davison expect to die and, if so, was it for that very reason that she pinned the flags to her jacket, to ensure the cause she represented would be discovered? Or was she hoping to stop the King's horse, however doomed the attempt, and then recover the flags and display them?

The interpretation of Davison's death still sparks a markedly divisive debate more than a century on. Her descendant, Geoffrey Davison, was adamant in his 2013 assessment that his great-aunt was 'not a mad woman intent on pointless suicide. Nor was she an intended martyr.'[66]

It seems certain that at the very least the suffragette intended to pull an attention-grabbing stunt to generate publicity for the cause. The Derby, as Britain's foremost horse race and one of the great dates in the national calendar at that time, was a canny choice of venue for such a stunt. It would not be the first sporting event, either, to be hijacked by the women's suffrage movement. Sports-related sabotage had become a popular tactic among the suffragettes by 1913. In April, for example, activists had damaged Ayr racecourse grandstand, causing around £3,000 damage. Cardiff and Kelso racecourses had also been targeted in vandalism and arson campaigns.

The spot at which Davison chose to intrude on the race-course also appeared far from random – it was right at the juncture where the horses broke into the final straight. She would have calculated that this was the best location to ensure her actions were captured on newsreel.

The presence of King George V and his wife, Queen Mary, was another factor that made the Derby an attractive platform for Davison. As well as drawing a great deal of press attention, which would be useful to her purposes, Davison perhaps also had in mind trying to influence the royal couple. The King, after all, was no friend of the suffragettes. Whether the action served to soften or harden his views about female enfranchisement, he would almost certainly have been left with little doubt about the seriousness of the suffragettes' purpose and the lengths to which their most militant advocates were willing to go.

It remains unclear whether Davison had actively targeted the King's horse when she stepped out on to the racecourse, however. Many suffragettes favoured the idea that she singled out Anmer from the field to make a statement. Most horseracing experts and historians have cast doubt on the idea, however. Michael Tanner, one such expert, argues convincingly that it would have been impossible for Davison to know if the King's horse had already passed her as she was standing by the rails on the inside of the bend at Tattenham Corner.[67] There was no public address commentary on the race, the crowds would have denied her an uninterrupted view of the horses and the speed at which the horses were running would have rendered it all but impossible from her close-up position on the rails to check if the jockey with the King's colours had gone past. He, along with scores of others, came to the conclusion that Davison's collision with Anmer was more a coincidence than a precise, premeditated plan.

Whether or not she could have selected the exact horse to approach, there is little doubt she was aware of the colossal risk to her life of walking out on the course. As one newspaper put it: 'To stop a racehorse in full flight is not a safe or easy proposition.' She was born in an age in which horses were ubiquitous: they were still the primary means of road transport. Some 300,000 horses worked on the roads and accidents were common. Moreover, a local hunt meet was stationed outside the house of one of her employers during her governess years. Although she is not known to have ridden herself, she would have been familiar with horses. Therefore the theory she planned to flag down the King's horse,[xxiv] before walking away unharmed, stretches the bounds of credibility.

She was clear-sighted about the danger into which she placed herself that bright June day and had spoken with increasing urgency in the run up to it about the need for a major sacrifice to put an end to the suffering of the suffragettes. In this light, then, can we view her act as one of martyrdom.

---

xxiv   It was the immediate verdict of many commentators in the aftermath. British Pathé put a title card on its shocking footage of the scene: 'Suffragette Killed in Attempt to Pull Down the King's Horse'.

Were all her motives so pure, however? It is likely that by this time she harboured personal reasons to be reckless with her life and health. Her spirits were no doubt negatively affected by the slew of rejections to job applications she had made in the final months of her life. More generally, a sense of exhaustion and frustration is detectable in her writing in the final year leading up to the Derby. It was also during this time that she learnt about the death of Reverend Forbes Jackson, the Baptist minister she had been charged with beating. A cutting of his obituary in *The Times* is said to have been found on her person at the Derby, suggesting she regretted the beating incident, or that at the least it played heavily on her mind. Unsurprisingly, contemporary commentators called into doubt her mental health, a charge passionately rebutted by her colleagues in the women's suffrage movement.

The Derby was the third time Davison had exhibited her willingness to die for the cause. She had told the *Pall Mall Gazette* newspaper after the iron staircase incident the previous June that that action had been a deliberate suicide attempt. Perhaps such rhetoric was easy to summon in the aftermath of such a painful ordeal in order to lend it the greatest impact. However, her sentiments were repeated elsewhere in her writing. She believed a 'tragedy' was necessary to advance the cause. As time went on and the vandalism and arson campaigns stepped up, her conviction grew that a greater sacrifice was needed.

In her essay, 'Price of Liberty', she set forth her conception of the 'perfect amazon, who will sacrifice unto the last for the freedom of her sex'. Discussing the comforts and qualities that a militant must give up in pursuit of their cause, she went on: 'The glorious and inscrutable Spirit of Liberty has but one further penalty within its power, the surrender of Life itself. It is the supreme consummation of sacrifice, than which none can be higher or greater.' While in hindsight it is tempting to assume Davison always had in mind the idea of herself as the perfect amazon, it is possible that she was referring in this essay to Emmeline Pankhurst. At last the feted WSPU leader was practising the militancy she preached, and was in and out of prison, undertaking hunger strike. She was in her mid-fifties and many comrades feared her escalating militancy and prison sentences would lead to her death. When suffragette Mary Richardson appeared in court in 1914 after slashing the famed Velázquez painting, the *Rokeby Venus*, in the National Gallery, she explained she had 'tried to destroy the picture of the most beautiful woman in mythological history as a protest against the Government for destroying Mrs Pankhurst'. She added: 'Mrs Pankhurst seeks to procure justice for womanhood, and for this she is being slowly murdered by a Government of Iscariot politicians.'[68]

With each passing month she became increasingly consumed by the idea that one grand gesture, one ultimate sacrifice, was needed. The calmness with which she had several times turned herself over to appalling pain and injury suggest her religious conviction, which underpinned her certainty in the righteousness of her actions, provided some comfort. In the end she found the strength to act upon the principle she had earlier espoused that 'one big tragedy may save many others'.

It is curious that, given her closeness with her mother, she left Margaret no note, farewell letter or explanation of her intentions. Perhaps it was too difficult to sit down in advance and commit to paper her plans and the complex emotions she felt surrounding them. And after all, it was also possible she would survive.

The stigma of suicide in preceding decades has influenced some commentators to argue that Davison did not mean to die at the Derby in June 1913. Several of her previous biographers also come to that conclusion. However, close attention to her writing and the trend of escalating militancy in her suffragette career led to another judgment. Her actions that day were deliberate and unless one wishes to accuse her of departing drastically from common sense, the risk to her life was obvious. She made a clear-sighted decision and it is likely that if she had survived this incident, she would have taken new risks that endangered her life. Davison harboured not a will to die, but a willingness to die.

CHAPTER 12

A HEROINE IN DEATH,
A MARTYR THEREAFTER

The suffragettes immediately claimed Davison as a secular martyr and, to them at least, it was clear that she would have stopped at nothing to further the cause of women's suffrage. The front page of *The Suffragette* on 13 June carried the strapline: 'In Honour and In Loving, Reverent Memory of Emily Wilding Davison'. The cover displayed an extravagantly winged angel in the foreground standing before a blurred illustration of racegoers. Inside was an admiring eulogy written by Christabel Pankhurst, who acknowledged that Davison's act was: 'A tremendous imaginative and spiritual achievement! A wonderful act of faith! So greatly did she care for freedom that she died for it. So dearly did she love women that she offered her life as their ransom.'

In its issue of 12 June *Votes for Women* was equally effusive in its appraisal of her final act, declaring:

Waiting there in the sun, in that gay scene, among the heedless crowd, she had in her soul the thought, the vision of wronged women. That thought she held to her; that vision she kept before her. Thus inspired, she threw herself into the fierce current of the race. So greatly did she care for freedom that she died for it.

Emmeline Pankhurst announced to the WSPU that Davison had 'given her life to call attention to the intolerable grievances of women'.

Her closest friends paid tribute to her in the pages of *Votes for Women*. She was deemed the 'most cheerful companion, the truest upholder of our Great Cause' by Constance Lytton, while Eleanor Penn Gaskell described her as 'one of the most wonderful personalities I have ever known'.[69]

Amid the grand rhetoric, elaborate plans were devised for a public funeral for Davison that would serve as a show of strength for the suffragettes. On Saturday 14 June her body was placed inside an oak coffin supplied by Furniss of Epsom, and taken by train to London for the ceremony. More than 3,000 women were waiting outside Victoria Station to greet the casket. Some of the younger suffragettes wore white dresses (with black armbands) and clutched white lilies – perhaps a signal of hope – while older Union members were clad in traditional mourning black and carried purple irises.

Davison's coffin was loaded onto a funeral carriage drawn by four black horses and the cortège started off down Buckingham Palace Road to begin its progress through the streets of the capital. A funeral wreath lying on the bier read: 'She died for Women'. Her close family, including her mother Margaret, sister Laetitia and half-brother Captain Henry Davison, the latter being named as chief mourner, travelled in a carriage behind, as did a 'Miss Morrison', tantalisingly described by newspaper reports as 'Miss Davison's intimate companion'. More than 100 years later her identity remains unclear, though several candidates have been identified by historians and scholars. Evelyn Mary Morrison, a WSPU activist known to have attended several of the same demonstrations as Davison was one possibility. Sybil Morrison, aged twenty in 1913, a lesbian and an ardent WSPU member who was once talked out of an act of militancy by Emmeline Pankhurst because she was too young to go to jail, was another. She became a prominent pacifist later in her life. A third candidate was a local Northumberland woman who was a younger companion to Davison during the stints she spent at home with her mother.[70]

Uncles, aunts and cousins were also present in the three carriages accompanying the coffin. Marching alongside it were Sylvia Pankhurst and five comrades, while eight young members of the Newcastle branch of the WSPU strode behind carrying lilies and bearing high a banner emblazoned with the Joan of Arc motto that Davison had claimed as her own: 'Fight on, God will give the Victory.' Emmeline Pankhurst, still ailing from the effects of hunger strikes, planned to join the cortège, but was arrested by plain-clothes policemen upon leaving her flat that morning with her nurse.

She was charged under the 'Cat and Mouse' Act, and taken to Holloway Prison. Despite her incarceration, she managed to send a note urging her fellow comrades to march on in the funeral procession with all the more determination. 'The government has decided that I may not join with the members and friends in paying a tribute of reverent gratitude to our dear, dear comrade, Emily Davison,' she told her colleagues. 'I am re-arrested. I return to prison to resume the hunger-strike. I shall do my utmost to uphold the standard of the revolt!'

Grace Roe, the suffragette who organised the funeral, had made provisions for a carriage carrying Mrs Pankhurst to take a prominent position in the procession. In her absence, the carriage was despatched with its empty seat, drawing attention to authorities' churlish refusal to allow her to attend.[71]

English writer Rebecca West,[xxv] who had only recently defied her family to join the staff of a feminist journal, later wrote in *The Clarion*:

> Many of the women in that funeral march were weeping; the sight of the broad arrows on her purple pall kept me from tears. Surely it was the most merciful thing that ever befell Emily Davison that her death, unlike her life, was unshadowed by prison walls … When I came out of the memorial service where, in our desire to testify that the way of high passion which she had trodden was the only

---

xxv The later author of *Black Lamb and Grey Falcon*, whose real name was Cicely Fairfield.

way, we had said and sung rather inadequate things over her coffin, I heard that Mrs Pankhurst had been re-arrested. And for a moment I was choked with rage at the ill manners of it. Imagine a government arresting an opponent simply and solely to prevent her doing honour to the body of another opponent!

Fifty suffragettes who had been hunger-strikers proudly processed, along with hundreds of others who had been imprisoned for their commitment to the cause of women's suffrage. Many activists carried banners bearing the Christian motto: 'Greater love hath no man than this, that a man lay down his life for his friends'. Other banners bore the quotation attributed to United States Founding Father Patrick Henry: 'Give me liberty or give me death'.

A large cohort of socialists turned out to honour Davison and show solidarity with the WSPU. Some postmen, who had been on strike at a depot in central London where Davison had set a letterbox alight, sent wreaths to her funeral. Herbert Jones's wife also turned up to pay her respects to the woman who, just ten days before, had endangered her husband's life at the Derby. WSPU branches around the country sent deputations to pay tribute to their felled comrade. The Gillingham, Kent branch of the WSPU dedicated a wreath with the message: 'She died that others might be saved from worse than death'. Other suffrage groups also offered tributes. The New Constitutional Society sent flowers to recognise 'a great act of sacrifice', while English writer and campaigner Israel Zangwill sent a bouquet 'From a Jew to a Christian Martyr'.

Not all allies in the battle for women's suffrage welcomed Davison's sacrifice, however. Philippa Strachey, secretary of the London Society for Women's Suffrage, wrote:

> This society is taking no part in ... Miss Davison's funeral. While respecting the fact that Miss Davison's action was done in good faith it is impossible not to realise that she risked the lives of many innocent people, and we deplore her actions. We have to realise that such an occurrence does great harm to our cause by alienating many people who would consider it right to give the vote to women but who do most strongly believe it is wrong to endanger the lives of other people.[72]

The WSPU's main rival, the non-militant NUWSS, also made plain their attitude towards Davison's action by declining to attend the ceremony or even send a wreath.

Several more patent signs of disapproval emerged on the streets. Bricks were reportedly thrown at the carriage carrying the suffragette's coffin by clusters of angry observers. Some suffrage leaders were meanwhile shocked to hear shouts of 'The King's horse!' and 'Three cheers for the King's jockey' called out as the procession passed by. Uniformed and plain-clothes police, fearing disquiet, hovered among the crowds, watching the suffragettes of the procession with greater suspicion than the cause's opponents on the margins.

Pockets of discontent failed to overshadow the great display of suffragette theatricality, however. With an estimated 50,000 bystanders watching, the procession took place accompanied by ten brass bands. Newcastle-born WSPU organiser Charlotte 'Charlie' Marsh, with whom Davison had in the past been arrested for rock throwing, was the cross-bearer at the front. Suffragette Elsie Howey[xxvi] was dressed as Joan of Arc, and sat astride a white horse as she accompanied the coffin. Eventually it arrived at St George's, Bloomsbury, where 6,000 women awaited. Some managed to squeeze inside the church, but the majority clustered outside. Sylvia Pankhurst later wrote of the day:

A solemn funeral procession was organised to do her honour. To the militants who had prepared so many processions, this was the natural manifestation. The call to women to come garbed in black carrying purple irises, in purple with crimson peonies, in white bearing laurel wreaths, received a response from thousands who gathered from all parts of the country. Graduates and clergy marched in their robes, suffrage societies, trade unionists from the East End, unattached people. The streets were densely lined by silent, respectful crowds. The great public responded to the appeal of a life deliberately given for an impersonal end. The police had issued a notice which was

---

xxvi   A member of the Young Hot Bloods, a secretive group of women under thirty at the heart of the WSPU, who made themselves available for 'danger duty'.

virtually a prohibition of the procession, but at the same
time constables were enjoined to reverent conduct.

That night, a suffragette guard of honour kept vigil, protect-
ing the coffin until it was, at noon the next day, taken from
the church and walked in procession to King's Cross Station.
There the casket was loaded onto the 5.30 p.m. northbound
train to Morpeth, via Newcastle. Curious onlookers gathered
to catch a glimpse of it at many stations along the way and
the train was said to have waited at each stop to allow the
convened crowds time to gawp or pay their respects. When
Davison's coffin and accompanying flowers arrived in her
hometown, it took an hour to remove the wreaths. In respectful silence, a crowd estimated to number 20,000 lined
the streets of Morpeth. It was a significant turnout given
the widespread antipathy towards the militant suffragettes
in some quarters of society. A letter printed some years earlier in the *Morpeth Herald* held that suffrage societies 'spoil
looks as well as manners, for their practices are conducive
of self-conceit, forwardness and evil emotions. That is why
women who become politicians in early life so seldom marry'.[73] However, the movement had won significant support in
the area by 1913, by which time even the market town's mayor
had become a member of a suffragist group...[74]

Davison's coffin was taken to the fourteenth-century
parish church of St Mary's on the edge of the village, where
Davison's father and infant sister lay buried. Folklore had it
that local suffragettes had at one juncture planned to arson

the church there in an act of militancy, but had been deterred after the authorities instated a guard patrol.[75]

The Benwell Silver Band played 'La Marseillaise' in honour of Davison's arrival. The song's triumphant call to arms, including the chant 'The day of glory has arrived', and its themes of tyranny, slavery and the idea of the common man as a soldier against oppression, captured the spirit of the occasion well. Unlike the public procession in London, nobody attempted to disrupt or ridicule the proceedings in Morpeth. The *Northern Echo* reported: 'Those who suspected it would be made an excuse for an abandoned theatrical display of political fervour were happily disappointed. The attitude of the crowd was most becoming and decorous.'

Davison's contemporary biographer, Gertrude Colmore, described her final resting place in minute detail:

> In the north country there is a little grey town, set in a basin of green hills. One of these hills bears on and around its summit remnants of a castle built and destroyed in bygone days; and on the shoulder of this same hill stands an old, old church, in a churchyard thick grown with yews and cypresses, with cedar pines and trees and shrubbery of many kinds.

Her gravestone bore the WSPU slogan: 'Deeds not words'.

The suffragettes continued with their militant deeds as 1913 went on. They escalated their vandalism of sporting facilities. Acid and spades were used to carve 'Votes For

Women' into golf greens in the Midlands and Scotland. Arson attacks became more frequent too: the clubhouse at Roehampton Golf Club was targeted and the grandstand at Hurst Park racecourse burnt down just a few weeks after Davison's death. Other attempts were made, with varying degrees of success, on buildings including Tunbridge Wells cricket pavilion, an Oxford boathouse and a stand at Preston North End's football ground. A suffragette was also arrested entering the All England Lawn Tennis Club's grounds in Wimbledon, south London, armed with paraffin and wood shavings.

In 1914, a year after allegedly witnessing Davison's fatal blow under the hooves of the King's horse, Mary Richardson suffered injuries in a strikingly similar context. She had gone to Bristol to throw a petition against force-feeding into George V's lap as he travelled in his carriage. In a bitter parallel with Davison, she was struck from above by the flat of the sword of a mounted police officer who cantered menacingly through the crowd on horseback. An angry mob jumped on her and beat her savagely. She was rescued by other police, but then thrown in prison, where again she faced the horror of force-feeding.

It was the outbreak of war in August 1914 that heralded a pause in the militants' campaign. The Pankhursts declared a ceasefire and passionately encouraged the suffragettes to aid the war effort rather than hinder the government. The Union moved away from anti-war sentiments and renamed its newspaper *Britannia* in a self-declared act of patriotism.

There was a fierce backlash against the move from some quarters, but in the end most suffragettes accepted Emmeline Pankhurst's call.

The war, which killed some 890,000 men, ended up leading in part to the first majority victory for the women's suffrage movement. In 1918, as the conflict came to an end, the government agreed to grant the vote to women aged thirty or over. The concession came after forty years of placid and respectful protest followed by almost a decade of aggressive militancy by the suffragettes.

The First World War had changed the social fabric of Britain, co-opting a million more women into the workforce and mostly into jobs previously done by men. While the popular idea that women were 'rewarded' for their war effort stretches the reality, it is likely that the patriotism of the suffragettes endeared them to both the public and the government.

It is often said the violence and militancy of the suffragettes deterred wider support for female suffrage and fed counterarguments to their demands based on theories of female lunacy and hysteria. It is true that the suffragettes lost support as their campaign became more aggressive in 1912 – we know that because it was no longer commercially attractive. From 1909 retailers like Selfridges had advertised in *Votes for Women* and high-end jewellers Mappin & Webb had sold suffragette-inspired designs set with amethysts, emeralds and pearls, to denote the campaign colours.[76] These initiatives noticeably tailed off after several years, however, as the suffragettes became more aggressive in their tactics and public opinion turned against them. Consumers no longer wished to associate with the cause so enthusiastically.

However, the militancy likely aided the campaign in some ways. It was, in part, a desire by the war-weary authorities to avoid a return to violence that prompted them to make a concession to the activists' demands.

When it came to it, the limited enfranchisement of women was not committed to the statute book via its own headline bill. Rather, it was a set of clauses appended to a bill designed to address a quirk in the law that required male voters to have been resident in the UK for six months prior to an election – a condition that could have disenfranchised tens of thousands of troops.

It would have taken another ten years until, in 1928, the Representation of the People (Equal Franchise) Act introduced true equality between women and men at the ballot box, reducing the voting age for all sexes to twenty-one.

In death Davison was adopted by her comrades as a secular martyr, meaning her calculation had paid off. Emmeline Pankhurst rallied her supporters, telling them: 'We are soldiers engaged in a holy war, and we mean to go on until Victory is won.' Emmeline Pethick-Lawrence also talked of fighting a 'holy war for women's freedom'. It was at the centre of this analogy with the crusades, then, that Davison resided as the suffragette movement's martyr. Edith Mansell Moullin wrote an anniversary tribute in the *Woman's Dreadnought* newspaper that set her friend's actions in this context.

She placed her among the 'martyrs all down the ages who have voluntarily laid down their lives for a holy cause', while Mary Leigh declared that Davison had 'been welcomed as a kindred soul by the heroine of old time, "Blessed Joan of Arc".'

Emmeline Pankhurst reflected later:

Emily Wilding Davison was a character almost inevitably developed by a struggle such as ours. She was a B.A. of London University, and had taken first-class honours at Oxford in English Language and Literature. Yet the women's cause made such an appeal to her reason and her sympathies that she put every intellectual and social appeal aside and devoted herself untiringly and fearlessly to the work of the Union. She had suffered many imprisonments, had been forcibly fed and most brutally treated. On one occasion when she had barricaded her cell against the prison doctors, a hosepipe was turned on her from the window, and she was drenched and all but drowned in the icy water while workmen were breaking down her cell door. Miss Davison, after this experience, expressed to several of her friends the deep conviction that now, as in days called uncivilised, the conscience of the people would awaken only to the sacrifice of a human life.

At one time in prison she tried to kill herself by throwing herself headlong from one of the upper galleries, but she succeeded only in sustaining cruel injuries. After that time she clung to her conviction that one great tragedy, the deliberate throwing into the breach of a human life, would put an end to the intolerable torture of women. And so she threw herself at the King's horse, in full view of the King and Queen and a great multitude of their Majesties' subjects, offering up her life as a petition to the King, praying for the release of suffering women throughout England and the world. None can possibly doubt that that prayer can forever remain unanswered, for she took it straight to the Throne of the King of all the worlds.

Christabel Pankhurst also wrote about Davison's death and its totemic significance for the cause.

Mother was ill from her second hunger-strike when there came the news of Emily Davison's historic act. She had stopped the King's horse at the Derby and was lying mortally injured. We were startled as everyone else. Not a word had she said of her purpose. Taking counsel with no one, she had gone to the racecourse, waited her moment, and rushed forward. Horse and jockey were unhurt, but Emily Davison paid with her life for making the whole world understand that women were in earnest for the vote. Probably in no other way and at no other time and place could she so effectively have brought the concentrated attention of millions to bear upon the cause.

Rebecca West also delivered an impassioned eulogy.

I never dreamed how terrible the life of Emily Davison must have been. Yet she was to me quite a familiar personality ever since I first met her just after her first imprisonment four years ago. She was a wonderful talker. Her talk was an expression of that generosity which was her master-passion … It was as though, delighted by the world, which her fine wits and her moral passion had revealed to her, she could not rest till you had seen it too. So I knew her, though I never spoke to her again. I saw her once more; last summer I saw her standing in some London street collecting for the wives and children of the dockers, her cheerfulness and her pyrotechnic intelligence blazing the brighter through a body worn thin by pain and the exactions of good deeds.

But for her last triumph, when in one moment she, by leaving us, became the governor of our thoughts, she led a very ordinary life for a woman of her type and times. She was imprisoned eight times; she hunger-struck seven times; she was forcibly fed forty-nine times. That is the kind of life to which we dedicate our best and kindest and their wits in ugly scuffles in dark cells. And now in the constant contemplation of their pain we have become insensible. When enlightened by her violent death, we try to reckon up the price that Emily Davison paid for wearing a fine character in a mean world, we realise that her whole life since she joined the Women's Social and Political Union in 1906 was a tragedy which we ought not to have permitted. For if, when we walked behind her bier

on Saturday, we thought of ourselves as doing a dead comrade honour, we were wrong. We were making a march of
penitence behind a victim we allowed the Government to
do to death…

> She longed not for a satisfying revenge, but for the
quickest end to the tormenting of her friends. And then
it was she conceived the idea of the need for a human
sacrifice to buy the salvation of women … We belittle her
if we think that her great decision can have made that
decision to die an easy one; her last months before death
must have been a time of great agony. To a woman of such
quick senses life must have been very dear, and the aban-
donment of it a horror which we, who are still alive and
mean to remain so, who have not even had the pluck to
unseat the Government and shake it into sense, cannot
conceive. And this decision was made by a soul harried
by a body whose state was such as would have killed the
courage in most of us. For the harsh treatment to which
she subjected herself was nothing to the treatment she
received from the prison officials, and between the two
her body was shattered … Till the day she died her spine
still hurt her. Twelve months of misery of body and soul
we inflicted on her by tolerance of this vile Government.

The WSPU went on to honour Davison with a fellowship
in her name and released a pamphlet in memory of her. The
Union also held a memorial service in Hyde Park in London
on the anniversary of her death in 1917. Mary Leigh kept and

cherished the WSPU flags that had been found on her person at the racecourse. She produced them at later demonstrations, including the Campaign for Nuclear Disarmament's Aldermaston march in 1958. In the immediate aftermath of her friend's death, Leigh is said to have devised plans for the Emily Wilding Davison Club, the Emily Wilding Davison Lodge, and the Emily Wilding Davison Pilgrimage to her grave on the annual anniversary of her death.[77]

Davison's death affected her deeply; she commemorated her friend's death each anniversary by sending flowers to her grave. By the time that Leigh died in 1978, however, Davison's grave had fallen into disrepair. It was restored to mark the seventy-fifth anniversary of her death in 1988.

Davison's sensational death made her one of the most famous women of the twentieth century, and her sacrifice has continued to shock and inspire new generations in the decades since the Derby. In 1999, Labour MPs Jeremy Corbyn and Tony Benn mounted a plaque in the crypt within Parliament where she hid during the census. She is also commemorated at Epsom racecourse, where a road has been named after her, and at Epsom Cottage Hospital, where another plaque has been mounted. Her grave in Morpeth is still a site of pilgrimage too.

A number of artistic projects, from *Emily*, an opera written by Anglo-French composer Tim Benjamin, to the play *To Freedom's Cause* by Kate Willoughby, have also been inspired by her life. On the centenary anniversary of her death in 2013 a festival was hosted in her name.

One other person did not forget her, either: the jockey, Herbert Jones. Life was tough for him in the years after 1913. Three of his brothers died on the Western Front in the First World War, and illness forced his retirement from racing at the age of forty-two in 1923. His prospects were severely limited. Yet Jones was a more thoughtful character than many might suppose, and the events of 4 June 1913 had stayed with him. In 1928 he attended the funeral of Emmeline Pankhurst. There he laid a wreath inscribed: 'To do honour to the memory of Mrs. Pankhurst and Miss Emily Davison'. In 1951, suffering from depression and grieving in the wake of his wife's recent death, he committed suicide. His family said that he had never got over that day at Epsom thirty-eight years before. For years, he told them, he had been 'haunted' by 'the look of horror on her face'.

That was his memory of Davison. History has tended to take the same view: focusing only on the suffragette's death. While it was her dramatic actions at Epsom and their fatal outcome that won her a place in the annals, her life bears remembering too.

APPENDIX 1

THE PRICE OF LIBERTY

D avison's undated essay was published posthumously in the *Daily Sketch* on 28 May 1914 and reprinted the following week in *The Suffragette* on 5 June 1914.[78]

The true suffragette is an epitome of the determination of women to possess their own souls. The words of the Master are eternally true:– 'What shall it profit a man if he gain the whole world and lose his own soul?'

And it is the realisation of this ideal that is moving the most advanced of the feminists to stand out at all costs to-day. Men as a sex have not yet grasped the inevitability of the forging of this last link in the chain of human progress. Ever since history peeps out of the mists of time the male of the race has made it his prerogative to give or deny the whole world to his partner, but has withheld from her that which is above all temporal things – namely, the possession of a soul, the manifestation of the Godhead within.

They have beautified and decorated the shrine, but they have kept it empty of the divinity which gave a significance to the paraphernalia of the shrine. Especially is this error noticeable and blameworthy in the latter days of the early Christian church, when it was seriously discussed whether women even possessed souls, and sufficient doubt on the subject was raised to condemn the sex from that time onward to an inferior position in the community.

For centuries people have been groping after the dry bones of humanity, forgetting the mighty spirit which alone could make those dry bones live, till early last century the sons of men saw the need of the vivifying breath, and one man after another, one class after another felt the quick stirring process, and rose to the wondrous life of civic freedom.

Could the partners of men be untouched by this marvelous awakening? Could women any longer remain dry bones merely or indeed even as a clod of earth in the valley? Could the newly aroused and enlightened race owe its origin to an insensate and unintelligent creature?

The wonderful renascence of freedom has to extend its kindly influence to all! In the New Testament the Master reminded His followers that when the merchant had found the Pearl of Great Price, he sold all that he had in order to buy it. That is the parable of Militancy! It is that which the woman warriors are doing to-day. Some are truer warriors than others, but the perfect Amazon is she who will sacrifice all even unto this last to win the Pearl of Freedom for her sex.

Some of the beauteous pearls that women sell to obtain this freedom which is so little appreciated by those are born free are the pearls of Friendship, Good Report, Love, and even Life itself, each in itself a priceless boon.

Who will gainsay that Friendship is one of the priceless jewels of life? Did not the Elizabethan philosopher remind us that friendship doubles our joys and halves our sorrows? Have not the poets sung the inestimable riches of friendship?

Yet this pearl is sacrificed without a moment's hestitation by the true militant. And, indeed, the sacrifice is inevitable, even as the sun puts out the bright glow of the grate fire. Yet the Lares and Penates are valued gods, even if lesser lights, whilst on the sunniest day a bitter frost may necessitate the worship of the lesser but more comfortable flame.

Thus the sacrifice involves terrible suffering to the militant – old friends, recently made friends, they all go one by one into the limbo of the burning fiery furnace, a grim holocaust to Liberty.

An even severer part of the price is the surrender of Good Report – one of the brightest and most precious of the gems in a woman's crown, as anyone can realise who knows how easily her fair fame is sullied.

Men have been able to go forward through good report and ill report, and so low has been the standard of morals for them that the breath of scandal but seemed to burnish more brightly their good qualities.

But owing to the same double standard the merest whisper of venomous tongues could damn a woman socially and politically, for to be safe she must be like Caesar's wife.

Hence, to women, reputation is often as dear as life itself. Yet even this jewel has been sacrificed by the militant, for she has felt the truth of the Cavalier poet's song –'I could not love thee, dear, so much, Loved I not honour more.'

And she has felt in her innermost soul that there was no chance of preserving any 'honour' worth the name if she acquiesced in a state of society wherein women's souls and bodies were bought and sold.

'Ye cannot serve God and Mammon.' What possibility for those who knew the existing evil to sit down and suffer it in comfort and peace? Better to be Anathema Maranatha for the sake of progress than to sit lapped in ignoble ease in the House of Good Fame! Better that all men should speak evil of her and revile her, fighting the eternal battle of glorious liberty and humanity!

But a more soul-rending sacrifice even than that of friendship and of good report is demanded of the militant, that of the blood tie. 'She that loveth mother or father, sister or brother, husband or child, dearer than me cannot be my disciple,' saieth the terrible voice of freedom in accents that rend the very heart in twain.

'Cannot this cup of anguish be spared me?' cries the militant aloud in agony, yet immediately, as if in repentance for having so nearly lost the Priceless Pearl, in the words of all strivers after progress, she ejaculates: 'Nevertheless I will pay, even unto this price'; and in her writhing asks what further demand can be exacted from her.

The glorious and inscrutable Spirit of Liberty has but one further penalty within its power, the surrender of Life itself. It is the supreme consummation of sacrifice, than which none can be higher or greater.

To lay down life for friends, that is glorious selfless, inspiring! But to re-enact the tragedy of Calvary for generations yet unborn, that is the last consummate sacrifice of the Militant!

'Nor will she shrink from this Nirvana. She will be faithful unto this last.'

APPENDIX 2

HER ONLY EXTANT SPEECH

'Nation's Need of Woman Suffrage—An Address delivered before the London Westminster and County Bank Lit[erature] and Debating Society, November 20, 1911', holograph manuscript written by Emily Davison.[79]

The speech, now held in the Davison archive in the Women's Library at the London School of Economics, was transcribed by Professor Carolyn Collette, an American academic and literary critic, for her 2013 collection, *In the Thick of the Fight: The Writing of Emily Wilding Davison, Militant Suffragette*, published by the University of Michigan Press.

Ladies and Gentlemen,

You have done me the honour to ask me to come here and put before you the nation's need of Woman Suffrage. The very fact that you are willing to hear what I have to say on the subject tonight proves that you hold this to be one of the great national questions of the hour. It is as

I trust that I shall be able to convince you, the burning question of the hour, the one round which pivots all other questions. There is not a single question in this country which touches men that does not also touch women, and for that reason in order that such questions may be fairly and adequately dealt with, the Woman's point of view is needed equally with the man's. The basis underlying the whole plea that I shall put before you is that of 'Justice.' Justice is my plea. Now Justice is a virtue which we value very highly in England. We say that 'fair play is a jewel.' We are proud of the sporting instinct which sets the quality high. Now there is genuine fair play among men, but I am here to claim it for woman. You have held it your duty to protect and provide for us in the past. But the storm and stress of life have so changed things that you can no longer do so. You must now afford us instead the shield of fair play, and you will be no less chivalrous in doing so. In so doing you will not only benefit us, but yourselves. For these chains whereby you protected us in the past, have now become to us chains of bondage. The cage in which the cherished songster was formerly tenderly cherished, becomes a cruel torture-chamber when no one is left to tend the prisoner.

Tonight however I want to deal one by one with the various aspects of our life, and to prove to you how necessary is this enfranchisement of women for the general welfare.

THE NATIONAL STANDPOINT

The favourite anti-suffragist argument against Woman Suffrage is that women's sphere is the home, and that therefore she must not enter politics. But to-day politics are entering her home more and more, and therefore if the home is to be safeguarded women must enter politics. It is a wellknown fact of present-day political life that politics are becoming more social and domestic in character, so much so that they are deliberately interfering in the relation between parent and child. Mothers are no longer allowed to know but [?] what is good for their children. They are being told by the state how to feed them, what kind of beds they must be put in, how to safeguard the children, and even lately what places they must not be taken into (such as the public house). Parents are no longer allowed to control their children's education, occupation and the like. Now of course it is quite true that the State may have a responsibility in these matters, but then if that be so, it is absurd for the State to exclude the woman's point of view. The rising generation is a tremendously important national asset. But then the mothers who bear the children have the best knowledge of their needs. May I quote as an example the question of Infant Mortality. In the papers on November 15th there is a very interesting account of the newly issued report on national health for the Local Government Board. What do we read there? In it the medical officer Dr. Arthur Newsholme gives proof of a ... disease, infant mortality, in 4 decades he quotes

Death rates per 1000 births
1871–80: 149
1881–90: 142
1891–1900: 154
1901–1910: 127

To what is this due? Dr. Arthur Newsholme says 'Even after full allowance has been made for the series of years during which climate conditions have been favorable to infant life, there can be no reasonable doubt that much of the reduction already secured—has been caused by that concentration on the mother and the child which has been a striking feature of the last few years. The amount of saving of life may be illustrated by a comparison of the average experience of 1896–1900 with that of 1910. In the latter year 897,100 births and 94,828 deaths of infants under one year were registered in England and Wales. Had the experience of 1896–1900 held good, there would have been 45,120 more deaths of infants in 1910 than actually occurred.' Is it not interesting and noteworthy that this decrease in Infant Mortality coincided with the rise of Woman Suffrage. I will go further and say that it is due to it. That I am not speaking wildly is proved by the Infantile Mortality decrease of Australia and New Zealand. Since women got the vote there, mainly due to the

fact that a very searching 'Pure Milk Test 'was made de
rigueur in those countries, and to the instruction of the
mothers in matters of hygiene. But it is not merely in
a question like this that it is so important that women
should have direct voice in the State. May I here quote the
striking words used by Mr. Lloyd George as an argument
for Woman Suffrage in addressing Women Liberals in the
Albert Hall on Dec. 5, 1908. He said: 'My conviction is
that you will never get really good effective measures for
housing, for temperance, or for other social reforms, until
you get the millions of women of the land to cooperate
in such legislation. It is for that reason that I am standing here to-day to declare that in my judgment it is not
merely the right of women, but the interest of all, that
you should call in the aid and the counsel the inspira-
tion of women to help in the fashioning of ... wish that
women had been altogether left out of the scheme until
they were able to put their points of view as electors. A
great outcry is now being made about the ... of the bill.
A protest meeting is even announced for the Albert Hall.
My two special cases I have now put before you. The fact
that for the national welfare women must have the vote.
May I before I leave this point add that women need the
vote to safeguard their position in national life as wives.
In the perfect house the husband and wife are helpmeets,
bearing each others burdens, doubling each other's joys.
The sacrifices, the privileges and responsibilities are not all
on one side, but on both. That is the happy home where

both points of view are expressed … there is large field of common human endeavor and experience to man and wife, yet also 'men are men, and women are women,' and for fair play both points of [view] must be ventilated. It is true that in the past an Englishman has claimed to be king of his own castle, a quaint commentary on the fact that home has been supposed to be the woman's sphere, and yet even there one did not rule. It is true that under those conditions there may have been outward peace, but what tragedies that peace covered and hid! If women had been really honoured as rulers of the home there could not possibly exist such terrible anomalies as the unjust divorce laws, the … about wife-beatings, the degradingly inferior position which the mother occupies … regard to her own child, of whom she is not the legal parent, unless it is illegitimate. Absurd laws about debts in marriage etc.

THE IMPERIAL STANDPOINT

I now pass on to a very dire Antisuffragist bogey that W. Suffrage means the downfall of the Empire. This argument is so insulting to Englishwomen that it is almost past enduring. Now the case which I wish to submit to you is this that the ideal of Empire is unity. Now unity cannot be obtained without a feeling of love and devotion. Why was the Rome [sic] a vast empire? Because at any date in her early days she understood this principle. Her colonies were encouraged to be self-governing and responsible. The highest reward to be awarded was Roman citizenship. And so she rose to the height of her power. It is in short the difference between her bonds of love and the bonds of brute force. That is the safest Empire which is grounded in the bonds of love. Which were the colonies of this Empire which came forward most readily when England was at danger in the Boer War? They were Australia and New Zealand, which are the most free. Why did Rome's Empire fail? Because she failed to remember that no Empire is safe however great and glorious if it is rotten within. Luxury and corruption had rendered her internally rotten. Now it is from that point of view that the woman's point of view is needed for the Empire. Of what avail have the greatest navy in the world, to be the greatest Empire, if the heart of the Empire is rotten? The very fact that the army and navy are ridelled [sic] with vice makes their glory a shame. Of what avail to pose as the champion of liberty when your women, the mothers of the race, are not free? Ye are sons of the bondwoman, not of the free.

This brings us to the next aspect

THE MORAL STANDPOINT

This nation cannot be a great and glorious one so long as there is a double standard of morality for men and women, which means in English that the brunt of suffering falls upon the weaker. How is it possible to talk of chivalry while such a standard exists in our midst. Now although the women undoubtedly suffer through this, it really hurts men the most. May I here quote Josephine Butler's words in her preface to Woman's Work and Women's Culture—'Whenever one class or set of human beings has been deprived of whatever just privileges or denied a legitimate share of God's endowment of the world, the class which suffers most eventually is not the class which is deprived, depressed, or denied, but that which deprives, depresses, and denies.' Remember this that the double moral code is a direct protection and encouragement of vice, and vice is always hurtful to the nation. It is in this case trebly hurtful, for it hurts the men, the women and the children. The extraordinary fact in this connection is that anti-suffragists are always telling us that men must rule because they are more self-contained, and self-controlled than women. Yet on the [other] hand, they will plead as the justification of this terrible double-code, that men are slaves of their penises. But that this standard will never be effectually changed until women are enfranchised is amply proved (1) by the life long toil of Josephine Butler to get the repeal of the C. D.[Contagious Diseases] acts (2) by the fact that at present no less than 6 Bills are before Parliament dealing with the question of this and the White Slave traffic and they have practically no chance of becoming law. That would not be the case if women had votes, because it is primarily the women's question. These are the bills— Immoral Traffic Procuration Disorderly Houses Prevention of Immorality Illegitimacy and Maternity Criminal Law Amendment (Infanticide) and they are as important for national welfare as any Insurance scheme.

THE FINANCIAL STANDPOINT

But I will venture a step further which will perhaps surprise my audience here. It is that it is of the utmost consequence for the nation from the Commercial Standpoint that women should [be] enfranchised. One of the root reasons of this is that the standard should be efficiency, but it is not that at present. It is cheapness. Women are cheap to-day. You probably know cases of women working as clerks, who work just as well as the men. Some say more conscientiously and painstakingly but they only receive ⅔rds the pay with what result? The men are being turned out of their work to make room for women, and the women are being ruined in body and physique by having to live on sweated wages. You all know the parallel inequalities in the Civil Service, where the Government leads the way in this iniquitous cause. You may also know that women inspectors receive less pay than men inspectors. Thus in the Civil Service ... You are well aware that the teaching profession is a disgraceful example of unfairness. In the N.U.T. [National Union of Teachers] for instance there are 38,380 women members to 30,693 men, they have to qualify equally, nay even more than the men, often have larger classes and receive less pay. Now all this is bad and unfair. It is indeed a national disgrace, and if it goes on must sap the commercial fibre of England, because wealth and efficiency are a national asset.

On one special feature of this aspect I must dwell. It is the Right to work. That idea with regard to men is coming forward very strongly. But what about women? Think of this legislation brought forward to close one avenue after another to women, till they are forced into the unskilled badly paid trades, or practically into the trade of marriage or domestic service. That is the only trade which no man seems anxious to take from women. But what about attempts to thrust married women out of factories or schools, the attempt on barmaids, florists, the printing trade in Edinboro' and last and most flagrant of all the Pitbrow Girls. All these various attempts would have excluded hundreds and thousands of girls from earning a decent living. And all the time the sentimental reasons are guises for taking away the women's work from them on the excuse that the work was unsuitable. When Mr. Robert Smillie acknowledged that he saw no harm in taking the work from the Pitbrow Girls to give it to old miners past work, we were allowed to see the cloven hoof. And as one of those women, one of a family of 4 who keep a decent house by the united effort of all in this line said: 'What is Mr. Smillie going to give us, when our work is taken from us?' In the latter case alone no less than between 5000 and 6000 women are affected. What will happen to them? May I remind you that Sir Frederick ... said to the Committee which passed that infamous argument, that if it were passed it would be an irrefutable argument for Women Suffrage.

THE SCIENTIFIC ASPECT

One of the most subtle arguments advanced against Woman Suffrage is the assumption that it means adult Suffrage and that this is doubtful seeing that there are more women than men. Now I have a very startling proposition to make here. It is this that you never will get a real [equality] of the members of the sexes until you have Votes for Women. On the contrary the disproportion will increase until you make the great change.

The suggestions that I have to put before you is this. If you study statistics of the rearing and culture of horses, cattle and poultry you will find that there is a curious law of nature which governs sex. It is that the offspring always follow the sex of the weaker side of the parents. If the male is the weaker, more males will result. If the female weaker, more females. This is a theory which I venture to put before you to night, and it is almost invariable too in the human family, personal observations will prove it to you. My remedy perhaps then is explaining itself. If we want more males to counterbalance the excess of females in our islands, we must develop and improve our women.

You know that women have already begun to improve in intellect and physique with greater freedom and opportunities. Compare the splendid race of English women to-day with those of 50 years ago. Well my advice is to encourage them to develop. Emancipate them in every sense, and slowly and surely your balance of the sexes will right itself, because more and more males will be born, who by the legislation dealing with infant mortality will live.

POLITICAL STANDPOINT

Finally, I come to the political aspect of the question. Only a few days ago Mr. Asquith exploded a bombshell on the nation in his announcement of Manhood Suffrage next year. You have not perhaps noticed it, but it is a fact that there is no outcry in the country for manhood Suffrage, in fact as Mr. Philip Snowden and Sir Alfred … have said you never so much as heard of manhood Suffrage until Woman Suffrage came to the front. We know quite well why. The open enemies of Woman Suffrage hoped to kill the woman's case by bringing forward that which might interest men the more, whilst the pretended friends of the Women's Cause hoped to filch the hard won success of the women to bring in Manhood Suffrage. We have known all along that our subtlest enemies were the so called Adult Suffragists. Well our fears are now proved true. Mr. Asquith is going to bring in Votes for all men to kill Votes for Women. You will perhaps remonstrate here and say that he has promised to keep his promise for the Combination Bill, and also has promised to allow the House if it so wishes to incorporate in the Bill a Woman Suffrage amendment, which will if it passes then become part of the Government Bill. My friends this is the most insidious form of attack to our cause. May I put it in plain language: He on the one hand declares that he will leave the House free to pass a non-party Concil[iation] Bill, on the other hand, he offers to allow Woman Suffrage to become part of a Gov[ernment] measure. Do you not see that by this act he has killed the Conciliation Bill? For us it is dead. It is now a danger—you ask why? Because an amendment on the lines of the Concil[iation] Bill, or of that with the Dickinson Amendment, including wives of electors, is dead against the bed rock principle of the WSPU which is that the women should obtain [the] Vote on the same terms as the men now have it or may have it. So long as men had a limited franchise, we were content to accept a limited one. But if their franchise becomes unlimited then so must ours or else it is an insult. Now the Government knows quite well that neither Womanhood suffrage, nor even Mr. Lloyd George's proposition have the faintest chance of passing into law unless brought in as part of the Government Bill itself. And that is why they have made this move, hoping to hoodwink us. Ladies and Gentlemen we are not to be hoodwinked. We have been playing at this game of political chess too long. We say that either the Government must add Womanhood Suffrage to be an integral part of the Bill, or else the Manhood Suffrage Bill must be withdrawn and another brought forward giving the Vote on Equal terms to men and women. The

Government refused us this on Friday last. We therefore have declared war. We consider that in so doing we are doing the greatest possible service to our country. The nation's need of Woman Suffrage was never greater. For consider what will be your position if Manhood Suffrage becomes law next year as Mr. Asquith declares that he intends it to do. You will have a completely male ascendancy in this country. The result will be disastrous in the extreme. If you want proof look at the United States and France. Both of these so called republics are riddled with vice, bribery, corruption, and bureaucracy. In America especially politics are so foul that decent men will have nothing to do with them. Compare these with Australia and New Zealand. These commonwealths of ours are the most progressive and enlightened countries in the world. The model for all the most advanced modern legislation is found there years before we made an attempt at it. Take for example their old age Pension Schemes, their surplus of Trades Board and Land Reform. The reason is plain because they are genuine democracies. For there the people are really sovereign, because it is the whole of the people and not one half only. I trust now from the reasons that I have put before you to-day that it is absolutely essential for the welfare of this nation that women as well as men should be citizens of their country, because you must be sons or daughters not of the bondwoman but of the free.

APPENDIX 3

'INCENDIARISM'
1911

HOLOGRAPH MANUSCRIPT WRITTEN
BY EMILY WILDING DAVISON[80]

This essay, now held in the Davison archive in the Women's Library at the London School of Economics, sets out her reasons for an escalation in militant tactics beyond breaking windows. She describes how she first set fire to a pillar box and the consequences of the offence.

The manuscript was transcribed by Professor Carolyn Collette, an American academic and literary critic, for her 2013 collection, *In the Thick of the Fight: The Writing of Emily Wilding Davison, Militant Suffragette*, published by the University of Michigan Press.

Unfortunately the manuscript is badly damaged with ink stains. Where there is uncertainty over illegible words, Collette has included a question mark. I have corrected obvious errors in Davison's punctuation for ease of reading, but have left her style intact.

A great protest was made on November 21 [1911] by the W.S.P.U. against Mr. Asquith's announced intention to bring in a Manhood Suffrage Bill in 1912, and his further expression of opinion that Woman Suffrage could be added as an amendment to that bill if the House so wished, but refusing to put it into the Bill himself, as part of the government measure. This was unpardonable, it was the last straw. The women held a demonstration in Parliament Square which developed into a wholesale smashing of the windows in Whitehall, the Strand, some West-End establishments and two newspaper offices. As a result arrests were made, and had to be taken at Bow Street day by day for three weeks. Sixteen of the cases were put to the Session, as the damage done was over L5. Amongst the others were Lady Constance Lytton and Mary Leigh. The former who had done well over L5's worth, was only charged with doing it to the value of L3.17s.5d. [?] and was treated most indulgently, in the court by Muskett and given a fortnight's imprisonment. Mary Leigh also had done nothing but defaced a [?] was ... system of as one of the most troublesome of the [?] and given two months. This made my blood boil. The injustice and snobbery was so great. However I thought that something would be done to avenge it. Nothing was done, and I resolved to take it upon myself to make a protest. This couldn't be done at once, as I was engaged in secretarial work. But soon I resolved to stake all. On December 1st, 1911 I gave notice to leave and began laying my plans. I resolved that this time damage should be done that could not be repaired. The next step to window breaking was incendiarism. On December 8th, when I was free, at lunch time I walked down the Strand to Fleet Street. When I arrived at the Fleet Street P.O. which faces Fetter Lane I calmly stopped at the big open mouthed receptacle for London letters, I took out of my pocket a packet of the same size as an ordinary letter. It was of grease-proof paper tied with cotton. Inside was some linen well soaked in kerosene. One corner of the paper was torn so as to let out the kerosene rag ready. To this I calmly applied a match, which I had struck on a box of matches, and held it for a second. A small boy was passing by and stopped short on seeing what I was doing. I let the packet, now well alight, go down the receptacle, and threw the matches afterwards. I then quietly walked on down Fleet Street and turned into the first Lyons I came to get lunch. My heart was beating rapidly, as I felt the boy might have given [?] of me, and also I did not know what would happen. After I had sat there a short time (about 10 to 15 minutes) I heard a long shrill whistle. This was followed by others, and still others. They were not cab whistles, they were too agitated for that, they were clearly police whistles. About 10 or so of these sounded, and I thought to my self that my object was accomplished and the letters now well alight. When I had finished lunch I went down Fleet Street …

into Fetter Lane. There I at once saw an oily [?] constable being spoken to by a plain clothes man. The thought at once flashed into my mind that the latter was instructing the former to keep his eye on the pillar box near. I turned down Fetter Lane towards Fleet Street when I saw facing me the P.O. I saw the telegraph boys looking at the very aperture down which I had thrown my packet and matches after. I rejoiced greatly, as taken into consideration with the other two [?], I observed that I had succeeded.

The next day I scanned the papers to see if there was any sign of the authorities looking for the perpetrator of the deed. That day I occupied myself with finding out the various penalties to which I was liable. I found that setting fire to buildings was an offence which rendered the person liable to heavy imprisonment up to penal servitude. But setting fire to post offices or pillar boxes or attempting to do so, meant a penalty not exceeding one year.

On the Sunday I occupied myself with putting my house in order, and with writing two print letters to the Press informing them that I had done the deed, that I expected the authorities were looking for the offender, and that I meant to give myself on Monday at 10:30, by walking up to the constable nearest to the Fleet Street P.O. and giving myself up to him. These letters I posted in a pillar box near St. Paul's, and then went in to service there. The service was curiously impressive, it was a Sunday in Advent and all was very solemn, and the sermon was to the fact that a glorious morning awaited the people of God.

On Monday I set out ready. I walked to Fleet Street. When I got near the P.O. I saw numbers of men, evidently pressmen, about. I walked up to City 185 [badge number] and said to him, 'constable, I set fire to this P.O. at 1:15 last Friday, and am ready to surrender myself.' He said to me, 'I know of nothing—I cannot arrest you.' Then 'I should not think of giving you such an advertisement for your cause. You are qualifying for Colney Hatch.'

Seeing I could do nothing with him, I walked into the Post Office, and asked for the Manager. They took me into the Lady Superintendent. She denied all knowledge of any such deed, and asked for my name and address, which I promptly refused her. Seeing that public authorities did not mean to prosecute, I walked away. Later on I phoned up the Press and explained what had happened.

The thought now in my mind was that I must carry out the protest so strongly that it could not be ignored. I laid my plans accordingly. On Monday night I did not go back to my rooms, but on Tuesday night I did. There waiting for me was a detective whom I at once detected. He was standing near my house and when I appeared he walked along parallel to me stopped and saw me go [?] in, and was there when I emerged a few minutes later. Now I thought of doing my protest on Wednesday night. Accordingly on leaving the place where I spent the day, I spent time dodging and … to make sure that I was not followed and then went off to some friends. I found that Wednesday night would not be a good time for my deed, and so resolved to do it on Thursday.

On Thursday morning I took a train to London. I got out in the city and walked Citywards, buying a box of matches as [?] I had six packets in my pockets. I meant to do as many pillar boxes which were easier to do undiscovered as were necessary, and then to go ... a Post Office in some very public place to be careful all fell out as I had arranged.

My first good chance occurred in Leadenhall Street. Half-way down it, going towards Aldgate, there is on the right hand side a large pillar box, on the pavement. This was an excellent chance as the mouth was round out of sight. I coolly took out a packet, lit it, held it a moment, and put it into the London [?] mouth. I noted that [?] pillar box would not be cleared for half an hour. Very much pleased I walked [here a large ink stain obscures rest of sentence] Then came into the Aldgate District and walked about there some time but decided to do nothing as the people [p. 6] were all of the poorer class. I ... at last to the Mansion House. In the wall of what I think is Poultney, facing the Mansion House and ... Webb is a pillar box let into the wall. I took out a packet, lit it alight. It flared up most splendidly, so that a man coming towards me saw it. He stopped and [?] most amazed, I feared might give me away to a police officer standing near by ... I also thought that probably he would be busy and not anxious to waste his time going to charge me and having to spend perhaps several days at police courts. My surmise proved to be right. I walked quietly up Cheapside. I saw a Putney Bus on the other side, crossed over, into it and went west. I went inside

248

and for some time did not feel comfortable for as the bus moved slowly. But when I got to Holborn I climbed up on top and began to enjoy myself. It was a lovely day. I got down at Hyde Park Corner and then walked to Harrods, and near there I entered a Post Office, and phoned up the London News Office as usual. They answered. I told them I was the Suffragette who sent letters to them on Monday. They were at once interested. I told them that I had made up my mind not to be done, that I had that morning fired two pillar boxes in the City ... that I next intend to do a Post Office ... asked them which they thought would be best to do it ... G.P. O. or Parliament Street [?]. They very agitatedly said they could not possibly give advice. Feeling amused and seeing the truth of this, for they would otherwise have been accessories to my act, I answered, 'Of course not I ought to have thought of that! Well! I shall do my deed to be caught at one or the other between 1 and 2 o'clock,' then rang off. I then went and had a good lunch at Slater's [?] near Knightsbridge and dawdled the time between 12 and 1 o'clock. At 1 o'clock I sallied forth. It was a glorious day and I walked to Hyde Park Corner. I looked at the clock. Time seemed to be going on, so I took a bus to Trafalgar Square. There I got down and took another bus down Whitehall. My reason for doing this was that if I walked down I might be spotted by detectives who would probably be on the look out for me and who might prevent me doing any thing at all. As I had said to the Press, I wished to be caught 'in the act.' My bus stopped at Bridge

Street. I got down. As I turned into Parliament Street, [?] I first came across Superintendent Wells, who looked at me curiously. I then came right facing Inspector Powell and Constable City 185, both in private clothes. They looked at me, but I was glad they were coming towards me, as they could not turn too ostentatiously. I however went on past them up to the Post Office. I stood there, and quickly took out of my pocket one of my kerosene packets, struck a match and lit it deliberately and put it in. That did not burn well, and I was not yet arrested, so I took out another and even more ostentatiously set it alight [p. 8] and tried to put it into the letter box. By this time Powell had seen what I was up to. He reached forward literally grabbed the thing out of my hand, blew it out, seized me violently and said, 'I knew you would do this, Miss Davison.' Cn 185 City seized me on the other side and they rushed me into Cannon Row Police Station. As we went I called out, 'I am arrested, friends.' They hastily led me along into Scotland Yard into Powell's own room, others following. There they took down particulars of me, and I told them that I had done two in the City first that morning. Looking uneasy, they asked me where. I said I would willingly describe the position of the two, and did so. They then went off to ask what the Post Office authorities wanted done, and I had a long chat with Powell, during which we discussed old events.

After about ½ an hour I was taken over to Cannon Row where several inspectors crowded around me who remembered me. One of them said. 'We have been quite expecting to see you in the House of Commons again.' I replied: 'Yes, I know you have,' having often 'detected the detectives' watching me. Another asserted that they had heard that I was married and 'had given it all up.' Presently they read a charge to me of putting matches and lighted matter into a Pillar-box in Parliament Street, and then took me off [p. 9] in a taxi cab with Mrs. Parson, the Matron, Inspector Powell and a Post Office Official. Arrived at Bow Street I was taken into the Matron's room, and found a strange one there. She was proved to be the sister of the one I knew. My case came on about 4 o'clock or so, before Sir Albert de Rutzen. I had heard it was Mr. Mershame [?], and was surprised when I saw the other. Powell read out the charges against me. When Sir Albert heard [?] them he said: 'Do you think the woman is in her right mind.' Powell replied, 'I believe so; she has been convicted many previous times.' He also said he might have [?] charges to bring up against me. Sir Albert then remanded me for a week to be kept 'under observation.' I was then taken back to the Matron's room, and by this time the gaoler had promised … through to my friends. In an incredibly short time two arrived whose numbers I had given, very dear old friends in the cause, and with them a young fellow, also devoted to the cause. They got tea in to me. I told one to get some luggage I had left ready, and to send it up to Holloway that night. Presently it was time to go in old Black Maria. I begged to be put near the door, and was [?] … I drove out of the yard my three friends cheered me, and I waved my handkerchief.

The odd incident of the old drive north was that the constable in the van turned out to be the very one with whom I driven just a year ago to Holloway in Election time. We went [?] again [?] first to Pentonville to let a wretched looking boy out, and I and another woman only were left. I asked her what she was in for [?]. She told me. It was the usual charge, 'soliciting', and she declared to me she had not been doing it. She looked a refined girl and spoke [?] with an educated voice. I said that I know that many of these cases were 'engineered' by the police to get conviction.

When we arrived at Holloway I [?] first got out and was taken into the reception ward, but they did not seem to know what to do with me. As I was waiting in the courtyard, my constable and I had a further chat. He said to me, 'You have only to breathe the word Suffragette here for them to be terrified out of their wits.' I laughed and replied that we had won this respect by sheer fighting and he replied that he knew. By that time they had made up their mind and took me off to the Remand / Hospital wing. Before I was put in my cell the Matron came to see me. We had a long chat about Strangeways (from which she has been [?] to Holloway), and then she put me into a cell.

This cell was large and airy (as the Matron carefully pointed out to me). It has a very fairly decent bed in [?]

it and decent wash-stand. It was next door but one to the one in which Mrs. Pankhurst had been in October–December, 1908. During my week there I had a very good time. I had hot water brought me in a basin in the morning, quite decent food, including fish and a pudding at mid day. Besides this I went to chapel service with the other Suffragettes. I had long chats with Mary Leigh. I also to my joy had a Suffragette next-door to me, who was a splendid companion. I was able to write 3 letters a day, and after a day or two got plenty of papers, and visits. In short I had the treatment which we all ought to have as political prisoners. I pointed this out to a visiting magistrate, who came in to see us at exercise on the Tuesday.

My next-door neighbour went out Monday, and like a regular comrade, went and looked after my … A newly formed society—The Men's Society for Women's Rights—on hearing that even a breath of suspicion had been raised against my sanity, determined to stand by me through thick and thin. Curiously, [?] a brother of mine, to whom I had written, came to see me and tell me that he would get his own solicitor to defend me. I was pleased and surprised.

At last December 21st arrived. It was a freezing wet day. I hauled my baggage along and got in a growler with two wardresses. We drove to Bow Street. We arrived punctually at 10 o'clock. I passed into the Matron's room. It was my old friend this time, who gave me a hearty welcome. Presently my good prison-comrade arrived to take charge of me, with some violets and white heather, and all kinds of nice things. Then my counsel and solicitor came in. We had a little consultation. I explained to them what I wanted done. My counsel, who was a firm Suffragist, understood at once. I knew he understood, for he confessed to me that he was always terribly worried on such occasions, for as a lawyer he wanted to get his client off, as a Suffragist he did not want to minimise the offence. Others arrived of my good friends, and soon after noon we went into court. I looked round to see the Court well filled with Suffragist friends. I saw a poor woman whom I did not know nod to me and say 'Cheer up.' I made signs to her that I was all right and smiled at my comrades.

The case proceeded. No … was made of my sanity. (I learned later that my counsel saw the letter which Sir Albert de Rutzen had received from the Prison Doctor to the effect that I was perfectly all right.) Powell gave his evidence and read my statements. My counsel put several very clear questions to him which brought out the fact that Powell had not been very accurate in his statements, for he declared that I was hiding from the public what I was doing, whereas my counsel obliged [him] to practically confess that I was not hiding it. P.C. 185 was also called, and the postman who sorted the Fleet Street bag on December 8th, who produced two packets found in the bag. The postman at Parliament Street was also called, and he testified to finding nothing in the bag, and gave evidence when he cleared the box. Then I was asked if I wished to say anything. I said I would like to make a statement and Sir Albert de Rutzen, after warning me that it would be used against me, told me to proceed. I began, but found I had to go very slowly, as the prosecutor was taking it down, and could only write longhand. He probably thought that would put me out, but it did not. Very slowly, loudly and clearly I said the following:

Gentlemen of the Jury,[xxvii]

I stand here for justice, although I feel that it is impossible to expect perfect justice in a court where every single official person from the judge to the public is composed of men only. Nevertheless I consider that I have a better chance of justice here where I am tried before '12 good men and true,' than in the courts where I have been lately tried where the prisoner could neither hear nor be heard, and where he was tried by a judge who was not in the most complete possession of his faculties. I mean no disrespect to English police courts but it seems to me that just as the country insists upon being served by men who are in their prime in the army and navy, so too it should be served by men in their prime in the administration of justice.

You have already heard the reasons why I felt bound to adopt this strong course. They were both cases of injustice, one a particular one, the other a general one. The particular one was the case of a great difference being made in

---

xxvii   Written separately from the previous narrative, in a much more formal version of her writing.

an English court between a woman of humble birth, and a woman of high birth. The other case, the general case, I had in mind to try to prevent England committing one of the greatest examples of injustice which have ever sullied her annals. I mean that all the males of the country should be endowed with the franchise, whilst not a single woman [?] was enfranchised, or if enfranchised was to be so endowed in a back-stairs way. Such an injustice would be flagrant, and would slur not only on the women, but on the men, who would be insulted by the refusal to treat their mothers as free women. This could not be tolerated and I trust will be avoided.

Then as to the act itself! Ever since the militant agitation began it is the women who have suffered violence on their bodies as a result of their demand for justice. At first they submitted, but as the violence grew worse and worse they realised that it was … to submit to this violence, for the women are the gates of life to the nation, and it was therefore tantamount to murder to allow the violence to go on from worse to worse. Hence the women rather than submit to it, preferred to use violence to property in order to avoid it. They first damaged Government property and you took no notice. They later damaged the property of the private citizen. But that could be repaired. And the [?] bodies of the women often could not be repaired. Three of my comrades have died for the violence inflicted on them on Nov. 18, 1910. I read in the papers the other day that the soul and honor of a girl child of 9 was valued in an

English court of law at 30 pieces of silver. The reference is obvious to you. I felt that I must do damage that could not be repaired.

Now as to the form which my protest took. It has been misrepresented to you here. It was an open protest. On Dec. 8th I dropped into the Fleet Street P.O. a pkt of linen saturated in kerosene, having set it alight. I threw my matches in afterwards and was seen by a small boy. I proceeded down Fleet Street and went into a Lyons for lunch—now for 3 proofs that I did something. After 10 minutes or qtr of an hour. I heard several police whistles. They were not cab whistles, they were too long and many. On finishing lunch I walked down Fleet Str. and came up by diverse ways into Fetter Lane. There I saw a plain clothes man giving instruction to a constable, it seemed to me about a pillar box nearby. As I came out of Fetter Lane facing the Fleet Str. P.O. I saw 2 telegraph boys looking down the very aperture down which I had thrown my missive. Yet at first it was denied that anything was done.[xxviii] As to the second case I determined to do two pillar boxes in the City which I accomplished. I then warned the press that I would do one to be publicly taken, and did so. Otherwise nothing would have been known.

Now as to motive, it was purely political—(Here interrupted by Recorder to say that did not concern Jury). Very well, I will keep to the question of guilt. Although

---

xxviii   In pencil above this line: 'yet afterwards I was charged with this'.

technically you may find me guilty, morally I am not. The moral guilt lies upon you the citizens of this country, who stand aside from the fight for the liberties of this country, and merely force the women to make protests how and where they may. We are … this country cannot possibly be genuinely democratic till the women, your mothers and sisters, stand side by side with you. Therefore the moral guilt lies upon you. I stand for the justice which you deny us.[xxix]

In address to judges in mitigation of sentence. I pressed the question of political motive said 3 things (a) to be allowed to pursue a vocation (2) not to be required to do prison tasks [?] and be able to keep … (c) to be allowed paper and letters, books, etc. … Pointed out I would and write book and asked to do so…

After I had finished the old prosecutor began to read it through. He mumbled frightfully, so in a very loud voice I called to him to speak up. He looked sick and [?] … 'shout if you like!' All through this trial and other trials I had been struck by the shocking acoustic properties of the Court, also by the way all the officials mumble from Sir Albert de Rutzen himself to the rest. Sometimes it seemed as if they did not mean the prisoner or public to hear, but this struck me as particularly unfair.

The old man mumbled on. When he came to the word 'decided' he apparently could not read his own writing and

---

xxix   This last sentence written in pencil.

hesitated as to whether it was 'deceive' or what ... in a very loud clear voice I told him it was 'decided' and spelt it to him 'd-e-c-i-d-e-d.' At this the court tittered and the gaoler beside me [?]. At another point I pulled him up for turning [?] two sentences into one, saying ... loudly: 'A full stop is wanted there, please ... the court was tickled.

By the way, when I made use of the expression 'incendiarism' in my statement, Sir Albert de Rutzen pulled me up, saying, 'One moment' (then addressing Mr. Cooper) 'is it at your advice that the prisoner is speaking?' Mr. Cooper, obviously ill at ease replied that he would rather answer that question in private. Then Sir Albert de Rutzen said 'I understand that she is proceeding on her own idea', and [of] Mr. Cooper that he [was] not able to prevent my speaking.

That bold statement of mine no doubt decided Sir Albert de Rutzen. He announced that the case must go to the assizes, Mr. Cooper said he could not oppose that. ... asked that I should be allowed bail Sir Albert seemed very unwilling to allow bail, but on being pressed said he would accept my own recognisances for L500, and two sureties for L250 each. I heard this to my great relief before I was hustled out of the Court. Afterward I learned that my counsel had the private interview with Sir Albert, who seemed very worried as to [whether] he had done right to let me out on bail. My answer reassured him on this point and [he] was to see a letter from the prison doctor stating that I was quite 'compos mentis.'

I went back to the Matron's room. My bail could not be settled up till the Court (which had adjourned for lunch) was sitting again and Inspector Powell could be present to accept the securities. All my friends came crowding in to see me and congratulate me. I was able to cordially thank my counsel and solicitor, and to learn who were to be my sureties. It was quite a joyous levee. My good friend, who had been my prison comrade for a short time and had moved heaven and earth on my behalf was there too with an excellent lunch which she had brought into ... After some minutes conversations it was decided that most of them should retire for lunch somewhere near the court, leaving me to eat mine with my faithful friend.

The Court was not to sit again till 3 o'clock. Just before then Inspector Powell strolled in, and we had an amusing three-cornered discussion, which went on for some time. At close on 4 o'clock, then I was beginning to wonder why I was still waiting for bail, one of my other friends came rushing into the matron's room with a declaration of joy and surprise at seeing this detective. 'We have been hunting and enquiring for you everywhere!' she cried. 'They were going to clear us out of the court' but we refused to go till you were bailed (turning to me). They told us you were not here (to Powell).' The others came pouring in and everyone was very indignant at the way they had been misled. We too were indignant that we should have been the unwilling instruments of the delay. A little while longer and it would have been too late to get me out on bail that night, and I should have been whirled away to Holloway. Then the bail would have been harder to arrange. In these matters Suffragettes have not been fairly treated, but it was Suffragette persistence which won the day, for my comrades had also refused to budge till I was released.

The ceremony of bail was soon carried out! I went through a passage with my two sureties, and undertook on my own recognisances of L500 to be present at the Old Bailey on January 10th, 1912, at 10:30 a.m., whilst my sureties each supported me to the tune of L250, and I walked out of the court to temporary liberty. After a joyous confabulation with my friends, I went off to spend two nights with one of my comrades, and next evening I started to go North to spend most of my short space of liberty with my dear mother. I was anxious as it was possible that I might be afterwards detained for some time at 'his Majesty's pleasure.'

NOTES

1   Gertrude Colmore
2   John Sleight (1988) p.28
3   Gay Gullickson (2008)
4   www.emilydavison.org/1911/03/index.html
5   Carolyn Collette (2013) p.8
6   Diane Atkinson (2018) p.73–74
7   Diane Atkinson (2018) p.74
8   Maureen Howes (2013) p.77
9   Michael Tanner (2013) p.170
10 Carolyn Collette (2013) p.29
11 Andrew Griffin (2013)
12 Andrew Griffin (2013)
13 WSPU pamphlet, http://spartacus-educational.com/WleighM.htm
14 June Purvis (1995)
15 Carolyn Collette (2013) p.141
16 Andrew Griffin (2013)
17 Andrew Griffin (2013)
18 http://www.emilydavison.org/index.html%3Fp=245.html
19 Andrew Griffin (2013)
20 *The Times*
21 http://www.emilydavison.org/1911/03/index.html
22 Maureen Howes (2013) p.81–82
23 Maureen Howes (2013) p.82
24 Carolyn Collette (2013) p.51
25 http://www.emilydavison.org/index.html%3Fp=148.html
26 http://www.emilydavison.org/index.html%3Fp=181.html
27 http://www.emilydavison.org/index.html%3Fp=357.html

28 Emily Wilding Davison archive in the Women's Library, London School of Economics
29 Carolyn Collette (2013) p.148
30 Carolyn Collette (2013) p.120–21
31 Carolyn Collette (2013) p.67–68
32 Gay Gullickson (2008)
33 Gertrude Colmore
34 Sylvia Pankhurst (1931)
35 John Sleight (1988) p.60
36 John Sleight (1988) p.68–70
37 Maureen Howes (2013) p.93
38 www.emilydavison.org/index.html%3Fp=179.html
39 Andrew Griffin (2013)
40 Andrew Griffin (2013)
41 Maureen Howes (2013) p.87
42 Maureen Howes (2013) p.88
43 Andrew Griffin (2013)
44 Maureen Howes (2013) p.88
45 Andrew Griffin (2013)
46 Maureen Howes (2013) p.55
47 Emily Wilding Davison archive in the Women's Library, London School of Economics
48 Diane Atkinson (2018) p.408
49 Diane Atkinson (2018) p.408
50 Diane Atkinson (2018) p.408–9
51 Gertrude Colmore
52 Diane Atkinson (2018) p.410
53 Emily Wilding Davison archive in the Women's Library, London School of Economics
54 Maureen Howes (2013)
55 http://www.historylearningsite.co.uk/the-role-of-british-women-in-the-twentieth-century/the-derby-of-june-1913/
56 https://www.britishpathe.com/video/emily-davison-throws-herself-under-the-kings-derby
57 https://player.bfi.org.uk/free/film/watch-suffragette-derby-of-1913-1913-online
58 Atkinson p.413, quoting letter posted 5 June 1913, private collection
59 Emily Wilding Davison archive in the Women's Library, London School of Economics
60 Emily Wilding Davison archive in the Women's Library, London School of Economics
61 Emily Wilding Davison archive in the Women's Library, London School of Economics
62 Emily Wilding Davison archive in the Women's Library, London School of Economics
63 John Sleight (1988) p.9
64 John Sleight (1988) p.10
65 Emily Wilding Davison archive in the Women's Library, London School of Economics

NOTES

66 Maureen Howes (2013), p.9
67 Michael Tanner, 2011 TV interview
68 Liz Stanley and Ann Morley (1988) p.164
69 Emily Wilding Davison archive in the Women's Library, London School of Economics
70 Maureen Howes (2013) p.12
71 John Sleight (1988) p.87
72 Diane Atkinson (2018) p.414
73 John Sleight (1988) p.60
74 Maureen Howes (2013) p.87
75 John Sleight (1988) p.70
76 Diane Atkinson (2018)
77 Diane Atkinson (2018) p.415
78 *The Suffragette* 5 June 1914, British Newspaper Archive
79 Carolyn Collette (2013) p.108ff
80 Carolyn Collette (2013) p.143ff

SOURCES AND BIBLIOGRAPHY

ARCHIVES

Hansard HC 28 Deb October 1909 vol 12 c1180

Police Sergeant Frank Bunn's police pocket book transcript in the Waltham Abbey Police Collection in the Epping Forest District Museum

Student register at Royal Holloway, University of London Archives

The National Archives: Papers of Emily Wilding Davison in The Women's Library at the London School of Economics (previously at the London Metropolitan University)

BOOKS

Abrams, Fran, *Freedom's Cause: Lives of the Suffragettes* (Profile Books, 2003)

Atkinson, Diane, *Rise Up Women!: The Remarkable Lives of the Suffragettes* (Bloomsbury, 2018)

Buckley, Mike; Harrison, David; Khadem, Victor, *Mapping Saddleworth: Manuscript Maps of the Parish, 1625–1822 II* (Saddleworth Historical Society, 2010)

Collette, Carolyn P., *In the Thick of the Fight: The Writing of Emily Wilding Davison, Militant Suffragette* (University of Michigan Press, 2013)

Colmore, Gertrude, *The Life of Emily Davison: An Outline* (The Women's Press, 1913)

Crawford, Elizabeth, *The Women's Suffrage Movement: A Reference Guide, 1866–1928* (Routledge, 2000)

Fitzherbert, Claudia, *Emily Davison: The Girl Who Gave Her Life For Her Cause* (Short Books Ltd, 2004)

Griffin, Andrew, *In Search of Emily* (ebook, 2013)

Harrison, Brian, *Peaceable Kingdom: Stability and Change in Modern Britain* (Oxford University Press, 1982)

Howes, Maureen, *Emily Wilding Davison: A Suffragette's Family Album* (The History Press, 2013)

Jenkins, Lyndsey, *Lady Constance Lytton: Aristocrat, Suffragette, Martyr* (Biteback Publishing, 2015)

Joannou, Maroula, *Ladies, Please Don't Smash These Windows* (Berg Publishers, 1995)

Kenney, Annie, *Memories of a Militant* (Edward Arnold & Co., 1924)

Lytton, Constance, *Prisons & Prisoners: Some Personal Experiences* (William Heinemann, 1914)

Mitchell, David, *Queen Christabel: A biography of Christabel Pankhurst* (MacDonald and Jane's Publishers Ltd, 1977)

Mitchell, Sally, *Daily Life in Victorian England* (Greenwood Press, 1996)

Nym Mayhall, Laura E., *The Militant Suffrage Movement: Citizenship and Resistance in Britain, 1860–1930* (Oxford University Press, 2003)

Pankhurst, Sylvia, *The Suffragette Movement: An Intimate Account of Persons and Ideals* (1931)

Pethick-Lawrence, Emmeline, *My Part in a Changing World* (Hyperion Press, 1976, reprint of 1938 ed. published by V. Gollancz)

Pethick-Lawrence, Frederick, *Fate Has Been Kind* (Hutchinson, 1942)

Pope-Hennessy, James, *Queen Mary, 1867–1953* (George Allen & Unwin, 1959)

Pugh, Martin, *Women and the Women's Movement in Britain 1914–1999* (Palgrave Macmillan, 2000)

Purvis, June, *Emmeline Pankhurst: A Biography* (Routledge, 2003)

R, A. J., *The Suffrage Annual and Women's Who's Who* (S. Paul & Co., 1913)

Richardson, Mary, *Laugh a Defiance* (George Weidenfeld & Nicolson, 1953)

Robyn Rogerson, Kristina, *Longhorsley Past and Present* (1990) http://www.genuki.org.uk/big/eng/NBL/Longhorsley/Past_Present

Rosen, Andrew, *Rise Up, Women! The Militant Campaign of the Women's Social and Political Union, 1903–1914* (Routledge, 2012)

Sleight, John, *One-Way Ticket to Epsom: A Journalist's Enquiry into the Heroic Story of Emily Wilding Davison* (Bridge Studios, 1988)

Stanley, Liz; Morley, Ann, *The Life and Death of Emily Wilding Davison* (The Women's Press, 1988)

Tanner, Michael, *The Suffragette Derby* (The Robson Press, 2013)

West, Rebecca, *The Young Rebecca: Writings of Rebecca West 1911–1917* (Virago, 1983)

ARTICLES AND JOURNALS

Ashforth, David, 'Horse Racing: Death at the Derby' (*Racing Post*, 2006)

Di Campli San Vito, Vera, 'Emily Wilding Davison', entry in *Oxford Dictionary of National Biography* (published online 2004)

Gullickson, Gay L., 'Emily Wilding Davison: Secular Martyr?' (*Social Research* Vol. 75, No. 2, Summer 2008)

Kay, Joyce, 'It wasn't just Emily Davison! Sport, Suffrage and Society in Edwardian Britain', in *International Journal of the History of Sport* (Volume 25, Issue 10, 2008)

Mitchell, Brian; Chambers, David; Crafts; Nicholas, 'How Good Was the Profitability of British Railways, 1870–1912?' (University of Warwick, 2009)

Purvis, June, 'The Prison Experiences of the Suffragettes in Edwardian Britain' (*Women's History Review*, 1995)

ABOUT THE AUTHOR

Lucy Fisher was born in Bath in 1989 and grew up in Wiltshire. She attended St Mary's School, Calne, before reading classics at University College, Oxford University. Her fascination with Emily Wilding Davison developed during childhood, after relatives living in the north-east claimed a family connection to the famous suffragette. She is now chief political correspondent at *The Times* and a regular broadcaster on the BBC and Sky News. She lives in London with her husband, Theo.

INDEX

'A Brief Record of My Life in Prison' 122–3

'A Militant on May Day' 154

Abbey, Lucy 26

Aberdeen Daily Journal 149–50, 151

Aboyeur 169, 172, 178, 180

Agadir 172, 175

Ainsworth, Laura 143

Anmer 168, 172–5, 176, 177, 185, 189, 195–6, 198, 200–201

anti-suffrage sentiment 83–6, 157, 231, 234

Ascot Gold Cup 186

Ashe, Thomas 70

Asquith, Herbert Henry 39, 44–5, 49, 87, 93, 94, 96, 106, 240–42, 244

Balls, Norah 139–40

Bell, Gertrude 86

Benjamin, Tim 221

Benn, Tony 221

Bermondsey strikes 100, 100n

Bishop, M. E. 28–9

Bishopsgate Institute 163

Black Friday 94–5

Boston Tea Party 40

Britannia 214

Bunn, Frank 169, 180–81, 189

Bunyan, John 119

Burt, Thomas 143

Butler, Josephine 236

Campaign for Nuclear Disarmament 221

Campbell-Bannerman, Henry 41, 44

'Cat and Mouse' Act 158, 208

census (1911) 97–8, 221

Chisholm, George Wilding 14

Chisholm, Sarah Seton 11, 12–13, 27

Church of England College for Girls 31–2

Churchill, Winston 34, 93n, 152

Clark, Mary 70, 95

Collette, Carolyn 229, 243

Colmore, Gertrude 16, 16n, 17, 60, 64, 72, 213

Conciliation Bills 44–5, 94, 96, 241

Corbyn, Jeremy 221

Craganour 169, 178–9, 180

Craig, Dr 131, 133–4

Daily Citizen 164

Daily Express 180
Daily Herald 43
Daily Mail 3, 41
Daily Mirror 44, 180
Daily Sketch 161–2, 184, 223–7
Davison, Alfred (brother of EWD) 14, 20–21, 153
Davison, Charles Edward (father of EWD) 2–3, 11–14, 20, 21–2, 26–7
Davison, Emily Wilding
    biographies 16, 19–20, 60, 213
    birth of 11, 14–15
    childhood of 2, 15–23
    commitment to women's suffrage 3, 4–5, 22–3, 36–7, 46–8, 49–50, 64, 110, 115–16, 139, 141–2, 154–5, 161–2, 190, 202–3, 205, 217–18, 223–7, 229–42, 255–8
    death of 1–2, 6–7, 9, 43, 61, 180, 185–6, 189, 191–3, 197–9, 201–4, 218–21, 222
    education of 2, 16, 20–23, 25–6, 27–31, 32–3
    and Epsom Derby 1–2, 6, 9, 61, 167–78, 179–81, 189–202, 204, 218, 222
    force-feeding of 4, 65, 67, 72, 74, 77, 96, 118–19, 120–22, 129–31, 134, 219
    in France 21, 153–4
    funeral of 7, 186, 206–13, 219–20
    health of 4, 53–4, 57, 74, 118–19, 122, 125, 128–31, 133–4, 135, 137, 140, 157, 159, 181–5, 220
    hides in Houses of Parliament 87–91
    hosepipe incident 73–80, 81–2, 217
    hunger strikes 4, 52, 53–4, 55, 56, 57–8, 65, 77, 96, 119, 122–3, 159, 219
    imprisonment of 4, 24, 50, 51–2, 53–4, 55, 56–8, 65, 67, 72–4, 81–2, 96, 116–123, 125–35, 153, 159, 217, 219, 251–3

    inquest 189–92
    iron staircase incident 127–31, 133, 135, 138, 156, 159, 160–61, 164, 202, 217
    joins WSPU 3, 37, 219
    legacy 6–7, 8, 9, 216–22
    letterbox firings 102–3, 107–9, 112–15, 138, 157, 209, 243, 245–51, 254–5, 257
    loyalty of 5
    'martyrdom' of 5–6, 7, 16, 43, 95, 110, 138, 156, 161–2, 185, 197, 201, 205–6, 216–17
    mental health 4, 122–3, 132, 133–4, 202, 253, 254
    militancy 1, 4–5, 7, 9, 22, 37–8, 49–51, 56–61, 64–5, 81, 92–3, 97–8, 100–101, 102–3, 105–8, 111–12, 138–9, 141–4, 145–52, 154, 157, 159, 161–2, 180, 243
    nicknames 17–18, 18n, 153
    ostracism from WSPU 4, 138, 140, 153, 160
    perfectionism of 17, 31
    physical hardiness of 24, 73–4, 140
    rebellious nature 4–5, 9, 16–18, 22, 56, 138, 153
    relationship with mother 94, 111, 138–9, 159–60, 204
    relationship with Pankhursts 4, 6–7, 102–3, 138, 153
    religious conviction of 5, 9, 15, 17, 19, 22, 51–2, 55–6, 61, 117–18, 155, 161–2, 203–4, 223–7
    role in WSPU 4, 45–7, 48, 49–50, 92, 138, 140
    and socialism 154–5, 163–4, 209
    speech to London Westminster and County Bank Lit and Debating Society 229–42
    and suffragettes' summer fête 164–6
    and swimming 24, 74
    teaching and governess roles 3, 31–3, 36–7, 42, 46–8, 201

Davison, Emily Wilding *cont.*
 and theatre 24, 98–9, 140
 writing of 3–4, 20, 36, 51–2, 54, 56,
  67, 71–2, 81–2, 86–90, 91–2, 96–7,
  98–102, 106–8, 117–23, 125–31,
  133–5, 140–45, 154, 157, 159–62, 164,
  202, 223–7, 243–61
Davison, Ethel (sister of EWD) 17,
 18–19
Davison, Geoffrey 200
Davison, Henry (Captain) (half-
 brother of EWD) 184, 190–91, 207
Davison, Letitia (sister of EWD) 14,
 27, 153, 207
Davison, Margaret (mother of EWD)
 3, 11, 12, 14, 19–20, 26–8, 48
 death of EWD 184, 185, 190, 192,
  207
 relationship with EWD 94, 111,
  138–9, 159–60, 204
Day Comet 178–9
Declaration of Tokyo (1975) 70
Despard, Charlotte 43–4
Diamond Jubilee 168–9, 177
Dickinson, Willoughby 163
direct action 3, 4, 7, 38, 49–51, 60, 92,
 100–101, 161
Donaldson, Dorothy 19
Dove-Willcox, Lillian 52, 52n

Edinburgh Castle 50–51
Edward VII, King 84
Emily 221
Epsom Cottage Hospital 177, 181–2, 184,
 190, 221
Epsom Derby 1–2, 6, 9, 61, 167–81,
 189–202, 204, 218, 221, 222
Ervine, St John 171, 172, 174

Faithfull, L. M. 29
Fawcett, Millicent 3, 8, 38, 40, 157
Field, Robert 164
First World War 9, 70, 214–16, 222

force-feeding 4, 63, 65–72, 74, 77, 96,
 118–19, 120–22, 129–31, 134, 141, 158,
 214, 219
Franchise Reform Bill 143
Franklin, Benjamin 56
Fry, Elizabeth 91

Gaumont Graphic 169–70, 175
George V, King 168, 177, 200, 214, 218
Gladstone, Herbert 76, 80
Globe, The 93
Gosforth House 140
Green, Alice 167
Grey, Sir Edward 34

Hardie, Keir 75–6
Harrison, Sir Brian 92, 103–4, 158
Havant, Gordon 76
Henry, Patrick 209
Hewitt, Harold 186–7
Hitchcock, Agnes 21–2, 23
Holloway College 25–6, 28–30
Holloway Jingles 119–20
Holloway Prison 51–3, 55, 69, 70, 96,
 104, 117, 118–23, 125–35, 138, 156, 208,
 251–3
Holloway, Thomas 25
Home Rule Bill 145
Horsley, Victor 69–70
House of Commons 6, 39, 44–5, 52, 55,
 76, 87–91, 93–4, 96, 98, 163
House of Lords 86, 87
Housman, Laurence 98
Howes, Maureen 19–20, 98
Howey, Elsie 211, 211n
hunger striking 4, 52–5, 56, 57–8, 63–4,
 68, 70–71, 77, 96, 119, 122–3, 158, 159,
 207–8
Hyde Park Rally 45–6, 163
'hysteria' 83, 84, 215

In the Thick of the Fight 229, 243
'Incendiarism' 106–7, 157, 243–61

infant mortality 231–3
Ismay, Charles Bower 179
Ismay, J. Bruce 179

Jackson, Rev. Forbes 146, 147, 148–50, 151–2, 195, 202
Jefferson, Thomas 56
Joan of Arc 5–6, 7, 56, 164–5, 207, 211, 217
Johnson, James 76
Jones, Herbert 168–9, 173–4, 175–6, 177–8, 179, 185, 190, 196–7, 201, 209, 222

Kay, Joyce 71
Kenney, Annie 34, 93n, 139
Kensington High School 21–3

Lamartine Yates, Rose 183–4, 190, 198
Lamartine Yates, Thomas 184, 190–91
Layland-Barratt, Sir Francis 42
Lea, Elizabeth 31, 32
Leigh, Mary 51, 59, 64, 65–6, 81–2, 105, 106, 114, 141, 147, 155–7, 164–6, 167, 171, 183, 217, 220–21, 244, 253
Lenton, Lilian 69–70, 104
Lloyd George, David 50, 58, 59–60, 61, 86–7, 105, 145–6, 148–9, 152, 233, 241
Loder, Eustace 179
'London equals New York' 144–5
London Gazette 27
London School of Economics 229, 243
London Society for Women's Suffrage 210
London University 31, 33, 190, 217
Louvois 178–9
Lytton, Lady Constance 'Con' 58–60, 63–4, 68–9, 74, 106, 114, 197–8, 206, 244

McKenna, Reginald 92–3
McNeill, Ronald 152
Manchester Guardian 75, 160, 173, 181
Manhood Suffrage Bill 106, 240–42, 244

Mansell Moullin, Charles 120, 182–3
Mansell Moullin, Edith 120, 146, 182, 216–17
Mappin & Webb 216
Marcus, Jane 54–5
Marion, Kitty 165
Marsden, Dora 81
Marsh, Charlotte 'Charlie' 98, 211
Marsh, Richard 197
Mary, Queen 168, 178, 200, 218
Men's Society for Women's Rights 253
Mill, John Stuart 99
MLWS (Men's League for Women's Suffrage) 183
Montefiore, Dora 39–40
Moorhouse, Edward 33
More, Hannah 92
Morning Advertiser 142, 143
Morning Post 100
Morpeth Herald 58, 212
Morrison, Evelyn Mary 207
Morrison, Sybil 207

'Nation's Need of Woman Suffrage' 229–42
National League for Opposing Woman Suffrage 85
New Constitutional Society 209
New York Times 172
Newcastle Chronicle 141
Newcastle Journal 141
Newsholme, Arthur 232
Nightingale, Florence 91
Northern Echo 181, 213
Nursing Times 160
NUT (National Union of Teachers) 237–8
NUWSS (National Union of Women's Suffrage Societies) 3, 37–8, 40–41, 138, 154, 157, 210

Pall Mall Gazette 160–61, 202

Pankhurst, Christabel 3, 33–4, 37, 43, 54,
    93n, 165, 193, 205, 218
    relationship with EWD 4, 6–7, 138, 153
Pankhurst, Emmeline 37, 105, 203,
    214–15, 216, 222
    death and funeral of EWD 197, 206,
        207–9, 217–18
    founds WSPU 3, 33
    relationship with EWD 138, 153
    splits in WSPU 43–4, 44n
Pankhurst, Sylvia 3, 37, 55, 145–6, 196,
    207, 211–12
    relationship with EWD 4, 6–7,
        102–3, 138, 153
Parliamentary Franchise (Women)
    Bill 145
Pathé Gazette 169–70, 175, 201n
Penn Gaskell, Eleanor 112–13, 116, 137,
    182, 183, 198, 206
Penn Gaskell, George 112
'People's Budget' 50
Pethick-Lawrence, Emmeline 43–4,
    44n, 70, 122, 216
Pethick-Lawrence, Frederick 44n, 122
Pilgrim's Progress 119
Piper, Edwin 178
pit brow women 101, 238
Powell, Francis 109, 113–14, 116, 250–51,
    260
Prisoners Temporary Discharge Act
    (1913) 158, 208
Prisons & Prisoners 74
psychiatric examinations 132–4
public opinion 7–8, 41, 43, 54–5, 71, 75–6,
    79, 104–5, 138, 212, 215–16, 231, 233–4,
    239–40
Pugh, Martin 68
Purvis, June 105

Racing Post 175
Reiff, Johnny 178
Representation of the People (Equal
    Franchise) Act (1928) 216

Richardson, Mary 132–3, 158, 170–72,
    174, 198, 203, 214
RMS Titanic 179
Roe, Grace 208
Rokeby Venus 203
Royal Commission on Divorce 84
Runciman, Sir Walter 59, 63, 64
de Rutzen, Sir Albert 251, 254–5, 258, 259

St Hugh's Hall 30–31
Sands, Bobby 70
Seabury School 32–3
Selfridges 216
Smillie, Robert 238
Snowden, Philip 76, 240
Stephen, Caroline 86
Stewart-Murray, Katharine 86
Strachey, Philippa 210
Strangeways Prison 57–8, 65, 67, 72–80, 81
Sullivan, Dr 119, 129, 131, 133–4
Sunday Times 36, 96–7
surveillance photography 104
Sutro, Alfred 98–9
Syme, John 144–5

Tanner, Michael 200–201
'The Anti-Suffrage Handbook of Facts,
    Statistics and Quotations For The
    Use of Speakers' 85
The Clarion 208–9
The Highway 163–4
'The Last Written Word of Emily
    Wilding Davison' 161–2
'The Perplexed Husband' 98–9
'The Price of Liberty' 7, 56, 184, 202–3,
    223–7
'The Real Christianity' 56, 117–18
The Suffrage Movement 103, 196
The Suffragette 71–2, 138, 165, 170, 171, 183,
    205, 223–7
'The Unexpurgated Case Against
    Women's Suffrage' 85
Thomas, L. Landon 32

Times, The 45, 69–70, 84–5, 93, 148, 163, 174–5, 180, 184, 191, 195, 202
To Freedom's Cause 221
Topical Budget 169–70

Vale-Lane, Jasper 176–7, 178
Victoria, Queen 35
Votes for Women 50, 75, 91, 98, 161, 205–6, 216

Wallace-Dunlop, Marion 52–3, 54
Ward, Arnold 83
Ward, Mrs Humphry 86
Webb, Beatrice 86
West, Rebecca 33, 208–9, 218–20
Western Home Monthly 141
Whalley, Albert 'Snowy' 187
Wharry, Olive 147, 147n
White, Gilbert H. 175, 189
White Star Line 179
Whitebread, G. 195
Whitman, Walt 155–6
Williams, Ethel 82
Williams, Henria Helen L. 94
Willoughby, Kate 221
Wilson, Laura 105
Winson Green Prison 65–6
Wolseley-Haig, Cecelia 94
Woman's Dreadnought 216–17
Women's National Anti-Suffrage League 83, 86
Women's Press 165, 165n
Women's Suffrage Bill 94
Women's Tax Resistance League 160
Wordsworth, Elizabeth 31
Workers' Educational Association 38, 154, 163–4
Wright, Sir Almroth 84–5
WSPU (Women's Social and Political Union) 55, 64–6, 92, 95–6, 102–3, 154, 164–5, 167, 241
    death and 'martyrdom' of EWD 7, 194–7, 219, 220–21

First World War 9, 214–15
    founding of 3, 33, 37
    funeral of EWD 206–7, 209–11
    Hyde Park Rally 45–6
    militancy 3–4, 37, 38–9, 40–41, 44, 44n, 49, 102–4, 141, 157, 203
    ostracism of EWD 4, 138, 140, 153, 160
    slump in membership 8, 157–8
    splits in 43–4, 44n, 81, 138

Yorkshire Observer 92
Yorkshire Weekly Post 100

Zangwill, Israel 210

37, 38, 39, 41, 44, 45, 51, 53, 54, 55, 59, 61,
71, 84, 85, 86, 92, 94, 95, 97, 99, 100, 104, 109, 110,
137, 138, 142, 143, 145, 146, 154 - 5, 157, 158,
160, 162, 163, 164,

bedrock, tumbril,
underestimate ! Vaudine.
Eddic edits.
untouchables · Anjula · grind·

* clarity of purpose
bolts of cloth. T-shirts

in 3 years 1) destroy - TM astonishing
most functional!
sentimentality
virtue signalling →

* R. Tusk, Diddy,